Jephthah's Daughter

PHILIP BEGHO is the author of several award-winning books. His wide-ranging interest has seen him in a varied career that has spanned journalism, banking, business, legal practice and university teaching. He has also engaged in film and theatrical production.

He now works as a full-time writer.

Verse Plays by Philip Begho

Esther

Daniel

Job's Wife

Jephthah's Daughter

Other Bible-based Plays

Jael

Joseph

Nebuchadnezzar

Solomon

Born King

Other Plays

Titi Rella

Traffic Jam Kids

Leopard Woman

Predator

Smallie

JEPHTHAH'S DAUGHTER

(Inspired by the biblical story of Jephthah)

PHILIP BEGHO

Monarch Books

JEPHTHAH'S DAUGHTER

First Published 2006

copyright © **Philip Begho** 2006
All rights reserved

All rights in this play are strictly reserved. No performance or reading of the play may be given and no copy of the play or any part thereof may be reproduced, stored in a retrieval system, or transmitted in any form or by means, electronic, mechanical, photocopying, recording, or otherwise, without the prior written permission of the author, with the exception of brief excerpts in magazines, articles, reviews, etc.

All applications regarding the rights to this play
(whether performing or otherwise) should be made
to the author through his publishers.

Cover illustration: E.O. Oludimu
Cover illustration copyright: Monarch Books

Email: monarch_books@yahoo.com
Tel: +234 8060069597

ISBN 978-37529-2-8

PUBLISHED BY MONARCH BOOKS
NIGERIA

JEPHTHAH'S DAUGHTER

JEPHTHAH'S DAUGHTER

CHARACTERS

JEPHTHAH, ruler of Tob, warrior, middle-aged.

SAHALIL, his beautiful virgin daughter, aged about 18.

AMIRA, an age-mate and one-time maid of Sahalil's, now best friend.

TAPUAH, lieutenant to Jephthah, aged about 28.

ABDA, a merchant and long-time friend of Jephthah's, middle-aged.

Maids, a Soldier, a band of Women and Children.

SCENE: •A lounge in Jephthah's house
•A lush and tranquil vale in Tob
12th century B.C.

Prologue

A lush and tranquil vale.

A darkened stage; lights grow to reveal the vale. A band of ten maidens, MAIDS *of* SAHALIL, *are in a circle covering* SAHALIL *from view.*

SAHALIL'S VOICE
As you have vowed, my father, so do to me;
Only give me two months to roam the mountains,
Weeping and bemoaning my virgin death.
[*The circle parts and* SAHALIL *is seen.*]

MAIDS
[*in dirge*]:
The tongue kills as surely as thrust of blade
Here – O here! – lies one slain by the tongue
Here is she killed by curve of mouth
Here is she slain by careless word
O here – here lies one slain by the tongue!

JEPHTHAH'S VOICE
Give your servant victory and Jephthah vows –
Your servant Jephthah vows, O God of gods –
Grant victory onto me and I shall give
The first, as burnt offering, O God – the first
From my house that comes to me upon my return!
Yes, O God – who comes first from my house
I shall give to you as burnt offering!

MAIDS
[*in dirge*]
The tongue kills as surely as thrust of blade
Here – O here! – lies one slain by the tongue
Here is she killed by curve of mouth
Here is she slain by careless word
O here – here lies one slain by the tongue!

JEPHTHAH'S VOICE
[*off*]
My daughter, is it you?

SAHALIL
[*half rising*]
What is it, my father?

JEPHTHAH'S VOICE
[*off*]
O woe! Woe! Woe is me!
[*Pause.*] I am Jephthah;
As I have vowed, so I must do.
I cannot take back my word.
[SAHALIL *rises.*]

SAHALIL
[*in dirge*]
Do to me, father, as you have vowed
For you are Jephthah
And I'm your daughter
Of the tribe that keep their word
Even to the death
Of the tribe that keep their word

That keep their word
Even to the death
Of the tribe that keep their word
Even to the death
Lo! I shall never know sweet wedlock
Never know the arms of nuptial warmth
But among the lilies
In the high mountain crags
A maid of maids
Virgin to the death
I shall roam
For I am of those that keep their word
That keep their word
Even to the death
Those that keep their word
Even to the death
[SAHALIL *lies down again.*]

MAIDS
[*in dirge*]
The tongue kills as surely as thrust of blade
Here – O here! – lies one slain by the tongue
Here is she killed by curve of mouth
Here is she slain by careless word
O here – here lies one slain by the tongue!
[*Repeating the dirge, they troop off the stage, leaving* SAHALIL *spotlighted as general lights fail. Then spotlights fail, with dirge still continuing. Then silence.*]

ACT 1

JEPHTHAH's *house. A lounging chamber, well-appointed, Middle Eastern, of its time.*

Two doors, extreme left wing (L) and extreme right wing (R), give to the chamber.

TAPUAH *pokes his head round (R).*

TAPUAH
[*calling*]
Amira…
[*He enters fully, looking about for* AMIRA.]
Amira… Amira!
[*He leaves, satisfied she is not in the chamber.*
SAHALIL *enters from (L), looking abstracted. She goes to some chests in a corner and rummages in them, but doesn't find what she wants.*]

SAHALIL
[*calling*]
Amira! Amira!
[*Enter* AMIRA *(L)*]

AMIRA
Yes, Sahalil?

SAHALIL
The parchments – I cannot find the parchments;
Father wants them – and the silver quill!
[AMIRA *dips her hand into a chest and brings out some parchments.*]

AMIRA
Are these what
Sahalil and Jephthah break their hearts for?

SAHALIL
[*taking them, embarrassed*]
Oh…

AMIRA
Right before your eyes, they were – begging notice;
And you couldn't find them…
[SAHALIL *clutches them to her breast and turns away.* AMIRA *approaches.*]
It's Abda, isn't it? The talk of marriage,
More than you'd care to say, troubles you, Sahalil?

SAHALIL
[*turning away*]
Marriage?

AMIRA
[*with a short laugh*]
Do you deny plans to marry Abda?

SAHALIL
Father hasn't given his consent.

AMIRA
But you know he will;
No better suitor could he wish his daughter
Than his friend of years, hearted pure and true;
And of purse, true-golden and full.

SAHALIL
I care not a hoot for gold's honeyed voice.

AMIRA
So they say
Who have never known the bite and sting
Of lack and want and wretched poverty.

SAHALIL
You know me, Amira;
Riches have no claw or fingernail in me.

AMIRA
But hold off, Sahalil, and tell me this:
Marriage, in maid and maiden a strong desire,
To rich and poor a thirst and hunger,
Comes to you in carriage decked with fire,
And at your feet meets not thanks but ire. Why?

SAHALIL
Not decked, sweet friend, with love's wonted fire.

AMIRA
Not with love's wonted fire?
Ah – you secretive, secretive thing you are!
Tending a flame for a prince unknown!
Now who is this prince of mystery?

SAHALIL
Oh Amira, you know there is no one.

AMIRA
Isn't there, my dear?

SAHALIL
Of course, there isn't.

AMIRA
There isn't?

SAHALIL
Amira!

AMIRA
[*gently*]
Yes, Sahalil?

SAHALIL
You're just being the silly girl you are.

AMIRA
Am I?

SAHALIL
There is no one – you know that!

AMIRA
Indeed?

SAHALIL
If there was,
Who would be the first to know but you?

AMIRA
Me? The hired help?

SAHALIL
Oh Amira,
You do get exasperating sometimes.
No more my maid are you, but my best friend!
And father is fond of you – you're family now!
[*Going off to (L) with parchments*]
Father waits; I must go. Do look for the quill;
You'll find it easily, I'm sure, as you found these.

AMIRA
[*when* SAHALIL *is at the door*]
Sahalil…

SAHALIL
[*stopping and turning*]
Yes?

AMIRA
Am I really your friend?

SAHALIL
[*turning to go*]
Oh Amira...

AMIRA
No, stop
[SAHALIL *stops*.]
If I'm your friend, your best friend, then hear me:
Don't blow away a dream chasing shadows.

SAHALIL
How can I when always, at the end,
I do what my dear father requires?

AMIRA
Yes – such obedience!
What end, I wonder, would come of it?
But now, let the blessings of obedience
Give grace to your face and call up a smile
As you find joy in doing what you must do.

SAHALIL
[*going off*]
And you, Amira,
Find joy in finding father his silver quill.
[*She leaves.* AMIRA *stares after her a bit, and then turns back to the chest to search for* JEPHTHAH's *quill.*]
[*Enter* TAPUAH. *As they talk,* AMIRA *occasionally interrupts her search with attentiveness to* TAPUAH.]

TAPUAH
Amira!
I have searched but everywhere for you!

AMIRA
Have you? Wonders multiply wonders!
[*Going to him*]
Well then, now that you have found me –
A kiss or two won't hurt the house of Jephthah.

TAPUAH
[*pushing her away*]
Have I heard right or aslant?

AMIRA
Ah, Tapuah has heard a thing or two!
Now, now, whatever can it be
That my true love has heard?
What have you heard, my love?

TAPUAH
Tell me, Amira: is it true, can it be –
Abda has asked for Sahalil's hand in marriage?

AMIRA
[*chuckling*]
Yesterday's crust, stale and cold;
Today brings hot bake: wedded they shall be.

TAPUAH
No!
[*Slight pause.*]

Jephthah's Daughter

So Jephthah's consent has gone?

AMIRA
No, he delays,
But only as a thing of ceremony.

TAPUAH
Amira – will you let it happen?
Will you let Sahalil marry Abda?

AMIRA
Why, my love, would I not let it happen?

TAPUAH
Amira! Abda could be her father!

AMIRA
So?

TAPUAH
But Amira…!

AMIRA
My love?

TAPUAH
Amira, the man is… is…

AMIRA
Yes?

TAPUAH
The man is old, agèd, ancient, antiquated,
Look – he is hoary-haired, full of gray years!
Damn it, girl, the man is old, old – *old*!

AMIRA
[*laughing*]
Again and again, I see youth,
Steeped in the strength of the early sun,
Mock as old the spread of the full-grown palm.
It cannot be – can it? – that noonday
Cannot see the many charms of evening,
But must scowl and glower with jealous fire
And call good old age old.

TAPUAH
It's easy to talk! Can you, Amira,
Marry a man old enough to be your father?

AMIRA
[*turning from him*]
I will marry the one I love –
[*Turning back to stare full in his face*]
Who has promised me marriage.

TAPUAH
What promise? It's void and holds no water,
But was born of passion, empty and mindless!
I just wanted… you know it, Amira! You know it!

AMIRA
Just wanted what? [*Chuckles.*]

Jephthah's Daughter

When a man wants, he simmers with passion,
Swears and swears and promises the earth;
When he gets, and to his fill has eaten,
All his golden vows he quite forgets
And turns and says, 'Pray, friend, of what speak you?
The promise is void and holds no water.'
Doubt not, Tapuah, on a day certain and true
You will cry hoarse to marry Amira.

TAPUAH
Is this time for threats and oaths,
When Sahalil's life stands imperiled?

AMIRA
What imperils it?

TAPUAH
Can it be that you cannot see?

AMIRA
I see what I see and see it full well.

TAPUAH
Will you be silent and have your benefactor,
She who raised you from servitude to honor,
Wander unhabored into misery's shoals?

AMIRA
[*laughs*]
What is Sahalil to you, Tapuah,
That concern should so deeply knife your breast?

TAPUAH
She is Jephthah's daughter.

AMIRA
Jephthah's daughter. [*Snickers*.] And?

TAPUAH
And nothing! If Sahalil's maid
Cannot for her mistress find loyalty,
Loyalty to Jephthah arms his lieutenant
With ready sword for war within,
As outside his portals on the battlefield!

AMIRA
War? Does marriage by Jephthah's daughter
To Jephthah's best friend, now in Tapuah's eye
Copulate to birth war for Jephthah? [*Laughs*.]
So pathetic is Tapuah! His tunic
Of noble nature has not cloth enough
To hide the breast of naked jealousy.

TAPUAH
Jealousy?

AMIRA
You are jealous of Abda, my sweet.

TAPUAH
Jealous of Abda – but tosh!
Why should Tapuah be jealous of Abda?

Jephthah's Daughter

AMIRA
Because Tapuah
Is mad with love for Sahalil.

TAPUAH
What!

AMIRA
Do I lie?

TAPUAH
What a mad and clownish notion!

AMIRA
Do you deny it?

TAPUAH
Mad with love for Sahalil!

AMIRA:
That a woman is silent, as I have been,
Bespeaks a tongue known to the blow
Of a husband's fist, as I will never know;
Or else declares the putting to bed
Of discoveries consigned to the rise
And shine of a gold-coined day,
As this day is.

TAPUAH
She to whom I have spoken but a dozen times?

AMIRA
Would that fool any but a foolish child?

TAPUAH
Mad with love for Sahalil!

AMIRA:
Who can hide calm and sober affection,
Much less hot and hopeless love?
The flutter of your eyelids, Tapuah,
The glance away from her,
The catching of your breath,
The softening of your voice when you spoke of her,
Were all the book of disclosure I needed,
To decode the secrets of your deceiving scrawl.

TAPUAH
Can any speak of love,
When words, the songbirds of romance,
Never found wings to soar in flight?

AMIRA:
Proofs true of feelings true, the unsaid words.
[*Chuckles as she continues rummaging.*]
How so easy to decode the hearts of men!
Not so easy women, yet Sahalil,
Like the infant she forever is,
Had her love, like baby food,
On brow and cheek and face!

TAPUAH
Her love?

AMIRA
[*laughing*]
Does your goddess
Disappoint you to show herself capable
Of so mundane a thing as love returned?
[*Finding the quill*] Ah… here is Jephthah's quill.

TAPUAH
Love returned?
[AMIRA *roars with laughter.*]

AMIRA
You couldn't see, could you, that with all she had
Of beauty, rank and wealth, Jephthah's daughter
Was but what she was – a woman!
And with a woman's passion to match yours,
Was crazy like hell for you, Tapuah!
[TAPUAH *moves to her thunderstruck. She points at him with the silver quill, amused.*]
But look at him – look at him!
[*Chuckles.*]
You loved her and she loved you, but neither knew
The other's love, and now it's too late;
She's as good as married and gone.
Too late, this fine and tardy knowledge –
Good only to torment and chasten you
For the infidelities of your heart.
[*Goes towards (L) chuckling.*]
And so I get to keep you, and to punish you,
And to be happy and thrilled by the thing!
Go nowhere, my sweet; I'll be not a moment
To Jephthah's chambers to hand him his quill.

[*She leaves.* TAPUAH *shuffles about dumbfounded; then breaks into sad laughter.*]

TAPUAH
She lies... She would drive me mad with lies...
Wonderful, wonderful lies! Sweet, marvelous falsehood!
Delightful, intoxicating untruth! Oh, my mind!
My mind has sprouted wings with sweet madness!
[*Enter* SAHALIL *(R).*]

SAHALIL
[*coming in*]
Amira, father waits!
[*Seeing* TAPUAH] Oh! You are here...
[TAPUAH *rivets his gaze on her.*]
I wanted Amira; where is she?
[TAPUAH *just stares silently at her.*]
Tapuah?
[*Pause.*]
Tapuah ... is there anything amiss?
[*Their eyes lock silently on each other for a while, then* TAPUAH *heaves a sigh and turns his face away.* SAHALIL, *disconcerted, inches backwards towards the door.*]

TAPUAH
[*turning to* SAHALIL *as she is by the door*]
Sahalil!
[SAHALIL *stops and* ABDA *goes up to her.*]
Sahalil...
[SAHALIL *looks up silently.*]

Sahalil... Abda... I hear...
Sahalil, has his suit found your hand to clasp?
[SAHALIL *turns away.*]
[*Pause.*]

SAHALIL
What is that to you?

TAPUAH
Sahalil...
[*He takes her hand gently and goes down on one knee.*]
Marry me, Sahalil.

SAHALIL
[*snatching back her hand*]
What!

TAPUAH
Marry me.
[SAHALIL *pulls back and turns away, breathing heavily.* TAPUAH *rises slowly to his feet and goes to her.*]
Sahalil...
[*She turns away.*]
My heart aches with love for you, Sahalil.
My first glimpse of you and I was stricken!
[SAHALIL *shakes her head in disbelief.*]
Sahalil...

SAHALIL
[*turning momentarily to him*]

You never said anything; never betrayed it.

TAPUAH
How could I?
One glimpse of you, and two arrows pierced me;
One, blinding love; the other, stupid dumbness.

SAHALIL
A hint, Tapuah; you could have given a hint.

TAPUAH
Sahalil, in your presence, my great love
Ever swelled from my heart to block up all my
    mouth.

SAHALIL
[*chuckles*]
And you didn't think to send a go-between?

TAPUAH
To Jephthah's daughter? If any knew but yourself,
The news was sure to get to Jephthah I thought.

SAHALIL
Where is he
Who said Jephthah's daughter should never marry?

TAPUAH
Oh Sahalil…

SAHALIL
And now the news you would not have Jephthah

hear,
Another has reported, and Jephthah readies to give consent.

TAPUAH
But Sahalil, you cannot let him do it.

SAHALIL
Why not? I cannot marry you.

TAPUAH
But Sahalil, I love you!

SAHALIL
And you love Amira too.

TAPUAH
Amira?

SAHALIL
Yes, Amira.

TAPUAH
Love Amira?

SAHALIL
Do I lie?

TAPUAH
[*chuckling*]
My lady, do you truly think
I could love that – that – I could love Amira?

SAHALIL
The way you both carried on, the things I heard…

TAPUAH
[*apprehensive*]
Who from?

SAHALIL
Your secret is safe;
Amira hasn't told anyone else, I'm sure.

TAPUAH
Be sure, Sahalil,
That if you heard aught from Amira
They were lies – lies, my lady! Lies!
I did some flirting – true! But my heart –
My heart never sat deep in it.

SAHALIL
But her heart did, it seems. Amira loves you.

TAPUAH
Amira cannot love.
Can a heart called Deceit, named Poison, love?

SAHALIL
Amira is my friend – you cannot speak thus!
[*Pause.*]

TAPUAH
The veil of innocence silks your face,
So you cannot know Amira like I do.

SAHALIL
[*defensively*]
She is my friend.

TAPUAH
Your maid.

SAHALIL
Once – but now my friend;
She has her quirks, I grant, but who hasn't?
Tapuah, you must never speak ill of Amira.
Now, I must go…
[*Begins to go.*]

TAPUAH
Sahalil, my lady, wait…
[*He goes to her by the door (L).*]
As you wish, I will not speak ill of her,
But you must believe me, my lady, when I say
What transpired between Amira and me
Was a silly little game of no consequence.
[*Enter* AMIRA *(L).*]

AMIRA
A silly little game of no consequence?
[*Shaking her head in pain*]
That I should live to see this day
When the snowy fields of my love
Should be strewn with the dung of farmyard beasts!

TAPUAH
Amira! If truth

Ever deigned to find soil in you, speak now…

AMIRA
Speak what? The truth? And so I will.
Is it not true,
Mighty lieutenant of Jephthah filled with slander;
Is it not true
You promised me your hand in marriage?

TAPUAH
Amira!

SAHALIL
[*turning to* TAPUAH]
You promised her marriage?

TAPUAH
It was vain speech! Empty!
She knows it; my heart was not in it!

AMIRA
But your substance was.
[*Rubbing her abdomen.*]
And soon will begin to kick.

TAPUAH
What!

SAHALIL
You… You are…?

AMIRA
Yes, my lady. I'm pregnant.

TAPUAH
No!

SAHALIL
[*her hands flying to her head*]
Oh!...
[*To* TAPUAH]
And you dared come to me? Oh! Oh!
[*Dashes out in tears.*]
[TAPUAH *and* AMIRA *stare daggers at each other; then* AMIRA *turns silently away. It is then* TAPUAH *speaks.*]

TAPUAH
That child is not mine!

AMIRA
[*with a short laugh*]
Then whose is it?

TAPUAH
It is a monstrous phantasm. A chimera!

AMIRA
When did Tapuah
Become a chimera, to breed its kind?

TAPUAH
It is the yield

Of the thousand men who have known you.

AMIRA
[*amused*]
So now, like a little boy, you seek
By insults and lies to unmake your deed?
Little boys who cannot stand like men
Should shun the games of the full-grown!

TAPUAH
You have ruined me!
Driven the love of my life from me!

AMIRA
So now the truth crawls out of hiding.

TAPUAH
She loves me!
I saw it in her eyes, her voice. She loves me!

AMIRA
Fat lot of good that will do now.
[*Laughs.*]

TAPUAH
Why, Amira?

AMIRA
Why what?

TAPUAH
Why do you hate thus – hate so?

AMIRA
Hate? Hate you?
[*Chuckles.*]
Can a woman hate the one she loves and will marry?

TAPUAH
To hate me I understand, for women hate
Where love is left pining. But to hate Sahalil –
To hate the morning dew caught upon a rose!

AMIRA
Morning dews and roses!
[*Laughs.*]

TAPUAH
A jewel matchless!

AMIRA
[*shaking her head*]
Only a fool thinks any woman a jewel.

TAPUAH
You hate, though you cover it;
Envy whips in you a hatred exquisite and
    unfellowed.

AMIRA
Envy?
[*Laughs derisively.*]
Though I confess a woman's common frailty,
And will gawk at the rare and wondrous gem,
I will not give bauble or colored glass

The pride and dignity of envy.
Revel in her deceit and false shining
All you wish, you and Jephthah – not so I!

TAPUAH
It is the eye of envy that sees deceit,
Or labors to find weeds and sundry ills,
Where no planting is but the wholesome stem
Of sweet purity and noble grace.

AMIRA
And what eye sees the rose's sweet petals
In the spike and poison of the ivy,
If not half-blind foolishness, the eye deceived?
[*Enter* JEPHTHAH *(L)*.]

JEPHTHAH
And what business has half-blind foolishness
Within the walls of Jephthah's reclining,
Or the eye deceived, or deceit itself?

TAPUAH
Greetings, my lord.

AMIRA
My lord, is it not this lieutenant of yours,
Once true, now false; once prudent, now foolish,
Who deceives himself and seeks a prize so high,
So far above the rungs of his office,
Latching on Jephthah's precious daughter
Eyes that dig where prudence ought not glance.

Jephthah's Daughter

JEPHTHAH
So the nuptial desires of quick Abda,
Giving the lie to years and silver age,
Have shamed youth and roused from slumber's belly
Green and tardy Tapuah to see Sahalil?

TAPUAH
My lord Jephthah is not incensed with me?

JEPHTHAH
Incensed? Why would Jephthah be incensed?

TAPUAH
But…

JEPHTHAH
But what? [*Pause.*] Ah, I see…
My once loyal buckler against men's venom
Has broken camp and fled my battlements
To join tongue with foes to hiss me names,
And call me irrational, easily incensed,
And ever brimming with red-hot rashness.

TAPUAH
Ah, but no, my lord…

JEPHTHAH
No? Then why think me to burn with wrath?
But of course, Amira speaks amiss –
You never did cast to see Sahalil.

TAPUAH
Never did cast to see Sahalil?
Oh Jephthah – you cannot know, you cannot!
But who with eyes to see can fail to see
The ruby, rare and precious, in the rose
That with dewy glory lifts its craning neck
Over a patch of drib-drab herbs?
And all the world is such a patch
Where you daughter, sweetest Sahalil, is.
That I cried not to you for the ruby –

JEPHTHAH
Was because you thought me irrational,
An ogre of rashness, easily incensed!

TAPUAH
No, Jephthah, no. That I cried not to you
Was because I lost my way in the blaze
Of the jewel's sweet and blinding fires,
With brain addled riotous by much surfeit
Of rending beauty and too-shining grace.
And now awake, if it be not too late –
And let it be not too late, Jephthah,
Let it be not too late! –
I throw myself at your feet to make suit
And ask the hand of my jeweled rose.
[*Throws himself at* JEPHTHAH's *feet.*]

AMIRA
Too late! Too, too late! Much, much, too, too late!

Jephthah's Daughter

JEPHTHAH
Rise, late one of a sudden agile – rise!
It is not at my feet prostrate you should be,
But before Sahalil on bended knee.

AMIRA
It is too late, Jephthah! Too late!

JEPHTHAH
[*gently*]
Has Amira become Sahalil's father?

TAPUAH
I have spoken with Sahalil, my lord.

AMIRA
Aha!
[*Enter* SAHALIL.]

SAHALIL
Father, Abda awaits you at the terrace.

JEPHTHAH
Is he back? So soon. What news bears he?

SAHALIL
Ammon bristles still for war.

JEPHTHAH
Blood! They want blood and shall have it – theirs!
[*Going*]
For we shall cleave asunder all Ammon's heart

To flood their cities and cavernous throats
With what their rabid thirst so endlessly craves.
[*He leaves.*]
[TAPUAH *and* SAHALIL *lock eyes a moment; then* SAHALIL *leaves.*]

AMIRA
[*with a mocking laugh*]
So what hope have you?
[TAPUAH *hovers about in confused desperation, silent.*]
[*Shaking her head*] Pathetic Tapuah…
Like a fly sweetly intoxicated
And all hopeless in the flagon;
Drowning – and drinking up all his drowning.
[*Enter* JEPHTHAH, *pulling in* SAHALIL.]

JEPHTHAH
No, no, my darling…
Give him ear, sweet or no, and let him speak.
[*He begins to go off, having deposited* SAHALIL *by* TAPUAH.]

SAHALIL
[*by* TAPUAH]
I have given him ear, father; I have.
And behold me, what for my pains scooped I?
[*Walking back to* JEPHTHAH]
A basket aswarm with monstrous catches!

JEPHTHAH
[*pulling* SAHALIL *back to* TAPUAH]

Give him second ear, my dear; second ear...
Lest the world should offer you the necklace of lies
They forged me, and cry, 'Like father like daughter!
Jephthah's child has learnt Jephthah's hasty ways
And wears her father's temper around her pretty
   neck.'
[*Walking to (R)*]
Come, Amira; find Abda some refreshments.
[AMIRA *does not budge.* JEPHTHAH *turns at the door.*]
Come!
[*Having glanced from* JEPHTHAH *to the two,*
AMIRA *saunters to* JEPHTHAH *and they leave.*
SAHALIL *and* TAPUAH *stand stiffly and silently for a while.*]

TAPUAH
Sahalil...
[SAHALIL *does not respond.*]
Sahalil... I ... [*Pause.*] Sahalil...
Sahalil, have no fear...
Nor will I further choke your ears with monstrous
   swarms;
No, I ask not that you marry me –
A toad Tapuah may be, yet not so beastly
A one to ask virtue's jeweled queen
To snuggle into Tapuah's toady filth;
For beholding now with eyes unmisted
I see I laid my bed with nothing
But blankets embroidered with dung.
No, Sahalil, let death visit, I say,
Ere you stoop to marry wretched Tapuah.

Yet permit me, Sahalil, my lily, my lady,
My rose delight, all a-bud and flowering
In sweet summer's dew and early glory –
Permit me to presume, my lady me,
To latch, if you please, on your beauty,
Yet not your beauty of form and mold,
Though that beauty, being a thing unmatched,
Is worthy of noble claim's highest call.
No, I presume not on your beauty of form,
But lay hold on your cast of spirit,
Being the crown of all beauties –
In you filled with grace and sweetness divine! –
And so at the foot of beauty's own throne,
Emboldened by the strength that freely flows
Where divine grace resides, I ask, Sahalil –
And how your name riddles me with music!
Sweet, sweet Sahalil; so sweet this music…
Yes, I ask, sweet Sahalil, for your hand,
Yet not your hand of marriage, but your hand still,
For I ask your hand of forgiveness…

SAHALIL
Forgiveness? Forgive your sins? Is Sahalil God?

TAPUAH
Repentant, I to God have run apace,
Asking forgiveness for a walk aslant;
And now with man offended, shall I dawdle?

SAHALIL
I pine with pain, perhaps; but offense?

TAPUAH
Did I not offend? Was it not offense
To nurture a love so full-bodied
That it could not slip frustration's grip
Till its bones and very spine escaped netherward,
And its body, all a formless mass,
All liquid, all dribbling, was ripe to find
Immorality's favored chamber-pot?

SAHALIL
Speak not so of Amira!
[*Long pause.*]

TAPUAH
I speak only of our deeds… but you speak true:
Deeds of swarming filth are deeds best forgotten.
Nevertheless, my lady, I cannot rest,
Nor will ease touch this brow, till you forgive.
[*Pause.*]

SAHALIL
If you would have it so, I forgive, Tapuah;
I forgive, though as I said, it is not this
Which pierces me – but pain;
Pain, Tapuah, not offense.

TAPUAH
My lady…

SAHALIL
My recoil from you, if truth be told,
Stemmed more from pain, than righteous pose;

For where love thrives most, pain quarries deepest.
Yes, Tapuah, you never knew, never dreamed,
But I have loved you with a love so deep;
Oh, so deep, so very deep, this aching love!
For deep did love's wound plunge and stretch
In the dark and endless well of silence,
Plumbing depths you will never know, my sweet;
For though I would this instant marry you
Were you free, duty to friend and child unborn
Bids me turn, and with heart slowly breaking,
Flee the span away from you of my love for you –
The stretch of heaven's face with space to spare.

TAPUAH
You would marry me if I were free?

SAHALIL
With no ado at all – no ado!
The fire that burns coy Sahalil
Flames for Tapuah not coyly or demurely.

TAPUAH
Behold me, I am of men most miserable!

SAHALIL
Misery hatched me first, ere it found your nest.

TAPUAH
[*raising palms stiffened in strangling pose*]
These hands – these feckless, felon hands…
Quick to stray to knead the breast of lust –
Will these hands – O me! – now find restraint

Jephthah's Daughter

[*Lifting hands to his neck*]
And fail to stray a little journey neckward?
Mourn! Mourn! O mourn the death of joy!

SAHALIL
Joy? Where cribs such a creature?
Where lives she but in empty summer echoes
Teased half-astir by the vagrant, idle breeze;
Now half-remembered, now clothed in mist,
Now swiftly drifting, now all-forgotten,
And never, nor ever, ever to recur!
[*Enter from (R) JEPHTHAH and ABDA talking.*]

JEPHTHAH
You know full well, Abda, that joy for me
Couches not in the thought that Gilead's house
Sues to makes me Prince, but fastens itself
In thoughts of victory over the foes of God;
Yet cannot I lie to pretend equanimity
At the sight of arrogance bending her knee
To give Gilead's firstborn his seized inheritance.

TAPUAH
[*going towards (R)*]
Greetings, Abda.
[*To JEPHTHAH*]
Permit me take my leave, my lord.

JEPHTHAH
And let amorous thoughts take leave too, Tapuah;
No time this for soft speech or tender play:
Ammon's sons wear a brow most defiant,

And to the clash of hard iniquitous speech
Are poised to add the iron of battle cries.
It's war now; but go, my lieutenant mine;
We will speak details in the auspicious hour.

TAPUAH
[*bowing to* JEPHTHAH] My lord.
[*To* ABDA] Sire.
[*To* SAHALIL] My lady…
[*A lingering look at her and he is gone.*]

ABDA
Amorous thoughts?
What amorous thoughts need Tapuah dispel?
[JEPHTHAH *breaks into laughter.* ABDA *turns to* SAHALIL.]
My dear, what conspiracy lingers here?
[SAHALIL *is silent.* ABDA *turns back to* JEPHTHAH.]
[*With growing anxiety*] Jephthah?

JEPHTHAH
Did you presume to think your eyes alone
Had brim enough to catch the sun's glow?

ABDA
The jeweled pendant trances the world's eye,
But deigns upon one breast alone to lie.
I was given to think –

JEPHTHAH
[*cutting in*] Think what?

What may a suitor unanswered think?

ABDA
But Jephthah…

JEPHTHAH
Had I given consent?

ABDA
Surely I was favored…

JEPHTHAH
That may be; but remember I cautioned,
I made clear that Sahalil, by obedience
To my wishes in all things, had earned
The privilege to vary my favor.

SAHALIL
[*leaving*]
Hold peace, father, I do not so intend.
[JEPHTHAH *and* ABDA *exchange glances.*]

JEPHTHAH
Sahalil…

SAHALIL
[*stopping at (L)*] Father?

JEPHTHAH
Did you speak aught?

SAHALIL
Have your way, said I, and stay your favor:
Tapuah's suit bent a hopeless, hapless knee,
And where it fell, there fell joy; there died all.

JEPHTHAH
His suit failed, is dead? Is it truly so?
Speak and say, my daughter; this man waits.

SAHALIL
I have said it. But I must go, my father.
[*Exit.*]

ABDA
O glorious day! O happy, happy day!

JEPHTHAH
True; happy this day that Jephthah's friend of years
Wins consent to wed Jephthah's precious daughter.

ABDA
Sweet the day! Yet I ask, is it true; can it be,
That Abda this day gains his heart's desire?

JEPHTHAH
No, not so.
[ABDA *looks at him aghast.* JEPHTHAH *chuckles.*]
What raw raving riot raids all your face!
But there is no cause for alarm, or perhaps there is,
For I jest and jest not: you see, my friend,
My consent remains unsealed – unsealed, Abda!
And a consent unsealed may yet be revoked.

Jephthah's Daughter

ABDA
So, today the dowry comes; today the sealing.

JEPHTHAH
Our custom, Abda! Our custom here in Tob –
The dowry on the day of the feast;
Only on the day of the feast, my friend!

ABDA
Our custom sits well on my brow,
Begging no nudge to remembrance.
Jephthah – I intend the feast today.

JEPHTHAH
[*shocked*] Today? *Today...!*

ABDA
A master of war, you bring men swiftly to arms
And at the snap of fingers, ready them for mayhem;
I, too, know the wings of the bird called swift
And in my mastery of the sea trade
Can call out a trading gain and profit
At the snap and time of a sail's unfurling.
The time till evening is all the time I need.

JEPHTHAH
We speak of nuptials and marriage feasts,
Not trading ships and profit.

ABDA
No greater profit may a man boast
Than to wed untrammeled grace and virtue:

Two names born twins to fair Sahalil.

JEPHTHAH
What can be rounded up now but breadcrumbs –
A feast unworthy of Jephthah and Sahalil!

ABDA
[*laughs*]
Abda's vats burst with wine and happiness;
His stores, with meats and seasonings from seven
    seas.
As for revelers – Tob's minstrels and men of
    prominence
Wait only for the sniff of festive hint
To color the tables of Abda and Jephthah
With honor and gaiety.

JEPHTHAH
No. Thoughts in dark and hooded garments
Now crowd and jostle me and would bear the light,
To unhood, of ponder and further reflection.
But hold this assurance: Sahalil is yours –
If you content me in the matter of the feast
Do you still propose the trip, friend, to Tyre?

ABDA
Tyre stands still, a royal palm in my thoughts.
But not alone now will I see that city of cities –
Sahalil would leap to see the sights,
And how refreshing to her the glad
And jaunty sea voyage would be!

Jephthah's Daughter

JEPHTHAH
Crammed and closeted for years in Tob,
She would be glad for the change and sea air.
[*Enter* AMIRA, *hastily going to* JEPHTHAH.]

AMIRA
[*stretching out a scroll to* JEPHTHAH]
Tell me I was quick.

JEPHTHAH
[*waving her off to* ABDA] Let him read.

AMIRA
[*going to* ABDA]
I snatched it as he bent to the correcting table.

JEPHTHAH
[*dismayed*] It comes with errors?

AMIRA
[*handing the scroll to* ABDA]
Errors? It was perfect.–
Perfect to any but our master calligrapher.
To him the symbol is flawed whose neck curves
With less sweetness than a swan's.

JEPHTHAH
And for that he would begin again.
[*Chuckles*]
Ehud will never learn: beauty is good,
Always good, but beauty overcrowds
The racing chariot of time and need.

AMIRA

[*waltzing over to* JEPHTHAH *as* ABDA *reads*]
So I spoke, though not in language as fine.
[*She wraps her arms round him.*]
My darling, would you have me repeat my speech?

JEPHTHAH

If I know you, Amira, it won't be fitting song
For the ears of our good man there…
[*The two exchange glances with* ABDA, *then* ABDA *lowers his eyes back to the scroll.*]

AMIRA

Hardly; but I had little intention
Of screaming it to the world.
A little whisper in your ear…
But first a little bribe…

JEPHTHAH

A bribe! Jephthah and bribes are sworn enemies!

AMIRA

Only one kiss this time, my dear; please!
[ABDA *coughs to interrupt them, but they just laugh and ignore him.*]

JEPHTHAH

What would mother say? I promised:
No kisses for the strange woman.
[*They laugh, then* AMIRA *angles up for the kiss.*]

AMIRA
Just a little one… Surely, mother won't mind…

ABDA
[*moving to them*]
But Sahalil will.
[*They pull apart.*]
It's a wonder that I alone know of this madness.

AMIRA
We have made Careful our very wrap.

ABDA
[*handing* JEPHTHAH *the scroll*]:
If your Careful boasts only a leaf for garment,
What will your Careless wear?

JEPHTHAH
[*gesturing with the scroll*] Is it okay?

ABDA
A thorough document.
[JEPHTHAH *begins to read.*]
The house of Gilead will not doubt Jephthah's terms
To battle and trample Ammon for Gilead.
But what are Jephthah's terms, his purposes
In his liaisons with Amira. Ah! –
There's a mystery hewn from dragon smoke!

JEPHTHAH
[*looking up from the scroll*]
My what?

AMIRA
Your purposes in your liaisons with me.
[*Laughs.*]

JEPHTHAH
[*laughing and moving to ink pot*]
Oh Abda…

AMIRA
I rather agree, if Abda means your purposes
Should come to roost in the coop of wedlock.

JEPHTHAH
Thoughts of marriage
Have made Abda soft anew
To inquisitorial righteousness.
[*He dips his signet ring in the ink pot and seals the scroll.*]

ABDA
You cannot deny
That my disapproval spoke always,
Even when Courtesy failed to dig.
[JEPHTHAH *hands the scroll to* AMIRA *to pass to* ABDA.]

AMIRA
[*going to* ABDA]
So Abda disapproves of Amira?

JEPHTHAH
Of our liaisons, my dear – not you.

Jephthah's Daughter

AMIRA
[*handing scroll to* ABDA]
So Abda disapproves of Amira…
[ABDA *turns silently to go and* AMIRA *eyes him.*]
Abda does disapprove. I always knew it, Jephthah.

ABDA
[*to* JEPHTHAH, *gesturing with scroll*]
Will you not change your mind? This is stuff
That should go from the hand of Jephthah himself.

JEPHTHAH
The house of Gilead shall not see this face!
No! Not till they stagger and beg
To cut covenant with the cast-off.

ABDA
[*turning at (R)*]
The other business, Jephthah…

JEPHTHAH
Dispatch this business;
Then shall matrimony be pleased
To have us sit at her table to parley.

ABDA
Indeed, my friend, and thanks.
[*Exit.*]
[AMIRA *goes toward (R).*]

AMIRA
[*barring the door*] What talks?

JEPHTHAH
[*of* AMIRA's *door-barring*] What is this?

AMIRA
What it looks like.
[*She goes to the other door (L), bars it, and waltzes seductively to* JEPHTHAH.]
We must not be careless – says righteous Abda.

JEPHTHAH
[*stepping away to avoid* AMIRA's *advances*]
We shall have to open should any knock,
And what a thing Jephthah-strange
To be caught sheepish behind closed doors!

AMIRA
[*angling up again to him*]
They would find only you; I shall be gone –
Breeze-swept through the other door.

JEPHTHAH
[*turning away*]
No, Amira; things unformed crowd my mind.

AMIRA
It's Abda – how I hate him!
He comes, and you draw cold away – always!

JEPHTHAH
He's a good man;
He could have tossed our secret to Sahalil,
But did not.

AMIRA
He would still – when they are married.

JEPHTHAH
Not Abda.
His secrets are tucked in the closets of forever.

AMIRA
So thinks Jephthah.

JEPHTHAH
So knows Jephthah.
[*Chuckles knowingly to himself.*] That man…

AMIRA
What tickles my lord?

JEPHTHAH
[*still chuckling*]
And he thinks none knows…

AMIRA
What?

JEPHTHAH
He and I are joined by more than friendship.
[*Pause.*]
His mother, like mine, kept a harlot's bed.

AMIRA
What!

JEPHTHAH
He thinks none knows.

AMIRA
His mother – a harlot?

JEPHTHAH
More notorious a one than she who bore me.

AMIRA
And Tob and the world know not?

JEPHTHAH
He fled her harlotry, the land of his birth,
When his years were like the morning.

AMIRA
You should have done the same –
Not waited for the snarl and cast off
Of brothers who claim purer blood.

JEPHTHAH
Running never did stave off Smirch.

AMIRA
It worked for Abda – if none in Tob knows but you.

JEPHTHAH
That may be; But not for me
The uncertain tents of hide and secrecy.
Jephthah would rather face the villain Smirch
In the open fields of dare and conflict

Jephthah's Daughter

Where all may see Jephthah's killing blow.

AMIRA
Wisely said; for the tents of secrecy,
Like all tents, are but spun with threads
Which fray with time to show naked loins.

JEPHTHAH
Let not this fray by your prating –
You must keep the man's secret,
As all these years I have done.

AMIRA
Have no fear, my dear;
Amira is Amira and no talebearer.

JEPHTHAH
Amira is but a woman.

AMIRA
Was it a woman who told Amira Abda's secret?

JEPHTHAH
[*embarrassed laugh*]
It was the trust I bear you, my pretty,
That curved my tongue to a place less than pretty.

AMIRA
Then let that trust hold your heart at rest.
[*Slight pause.*] And he doesn't know you know?

JEPHTHAH
Not the slightest hint has slipped my lips to him.

AMIRA
[*advancing seductively*]
Your righteous friend –
Nothing but a harlot's whelp…

JEPHTHAH
[*shaking his head*]
Oh! Would I hadn't spoken so of noble Abda!

AMIRA
You trust me not.

JEPHTHAH
No word of this must slip your lips, Amira!

AMIRA
No word will.
Would I be panting for the sweetness of a kiss
If my mind hung still with bat-coves
Of Abda's unpretty secret?

JEPHTHAH
[*turning from her advances*]
But the bats of war plague me heavy.

AMIRA
Since when did war sue to unmake Jephthah –
The mighty Jephthah forged in the womb of war?

JEPHTHAH
This war heaves like none other;
More than life is threatened.

AMIRA
What can be more than life?

JEPHTHAH
Ambition.

AMIRA
Ambition?

JEPHTHAH
If ambition achieves, it lives – when life has died.

AMIRA
In the hack and slash of ambition,
Jephthah has conquered foes round about
And found plunder and riches for himself;
What more would Jephthah have ambition give?

JEPHTHAH
Honor.

AMIRA
Honor? In Tob you are lord and master
And trail a robe enveined with men's respect.

JEPHTHAH
In Tob – the land of my exile. Tob is Tob;
Israel, Israel – and there in my birthplace,

In the house of my father Gilead,
In the hearts of my brothers and kinsmen,
I am but dung, a harlot's vomit!

AMIRA
No. No more so. Gilead now clamors to you
To unmake Ammon, and would make you Prince –
Prince in the noble house of Gilead –
When the war is done and Ammon slain,
And peace like dew covers the land again.

JEPHTHAH
When the war is done…
When Jephthah has won the war for Gilead…
[*Pause.*]
Amira – and should Jephthah not win?

AMIRA
What? Not win?

JEPHTHAH
Yes.

AMIRA
Why would Jephthah sue to not win?

JEPHTHAH
I am but a man; God alone
Knows the dwelling place of success perennial.

AMIRA
You forget –

Jephthah's Daughter

No war has seen Jephthah's back to the ground,
Weeping the skies for mercy or help.

JEPHTHAH
You forget Kidron-Baal and Merah-Kadesh.

AMIRA
No war those – but frays, petty skirmishes.
You took them unready, with no vows uttered –
So said you yourself – and so you lost.
But the wars and mammoth battles you undertook
With vows and oaths and serious swearing,
You never lost. Why would this be different?

JEPHTHAH
If God would but give me victory!

AMIRA
He has never failed you.

JEPHTHAH
If He would but give victory…

AMIRA
Trust Him…

JEPHTHAH
O God! O God! God of my fathers! –
The God of Abraham, Isaac and Jacob!
You have been the forge and strength of my arm! –
Have taught me to bend the bow of bronze!
Have given me invincible steel for wrist!

Have wrought in my heart iron valor!
O God of my fathers, I bow and worship!
[*Kneels and bows head to the ground, then raises face.*]
You have made me the scourge of your enemies,
Have made me a battle-ax on your foes
And brought me in song from a thousand battles!
Now I beseech you, hear me, O King of Heaven,
And grant me the song of victory once again!
Go before me like a consuming fire,
Wreaking havoc and marvelous destruction
Against the sons and hirelings of Ammon
Who rage against your people and defile your Name!
Give your servant victory and Jephthah vows –
Your servant Jephthah vows, O God of gods –
Grant victory unto me and I shall give
The first, as burnt offering, O God – the first
From my house that comes to me upon my return!
Yes, O God – who comes first from my house
I shall give to you as burnt offering!
[*Rising to his feet.*]
I thank you, O God, for victory is mine!

AMIRA
Jephthah!

JEPHTHAH
[*going to (L)*]
I have no time, Amira, for your tattle.
War, like fire, circles my brow with burning.

Jephthah's Daughter

AMIRA
But Jephthah!

JEPHTHAH
Unbar the doors.

AMIRA
[*going to him*]
Has your God become a dragon of blood
Waiting in hiding for sacrifices
Of innocents and the sweet unwary?

JEPHTHAH
[*waiting at door*] Unbar this door!
[AMIRA *unbars the door and* JEPHTHAH *storms out.*]

AMIRA
[*shaking her head*]
Never, O never did man a rasher vow make!
[*Going to unbar door (R)*]
Did his God who honored ever his unmad vows
Now need his madness to do him and Gilead good?
[*Approaching the audience, having unbarred (R)*]
But what need I lament? What bewail?
When Jephthah from war returns victorious
Will he find Amira first to burn?
[*Pause. Her face softens into a smile. She chuckles.*]
Who more fitting to greet Jephthah first?
Pray, speak – who?
[*Pause.*] And so with one little tug,
I shall pluck down the petal of my envy,

Unfix the root of the one I hate,
And win me the rose of my tender love!
[*Turning and heading for (R)*]
Rashness – what sweet uses teem in you!
Encircle and embrace me ever!
[TAPUAH *barges in before she can go out.*]

TAPUAH
Aha, Amira –
Come! We must press this thing further!

AMIRA
[*sidestepping and continuing on her way*]
No time, my love, for presses and sweet play.
[*Exit.*]

TAPUAH
[*rooted to the spot*]
 Amira!
[*He begins to go after her.*]

AMIRA
[*returning*]
But no –
I sniff the turn of profit in a pause here.

TAPUAH
Amira – you must help me!
My mind heaves to destruction!

AMIRA
Now? When war bares its teeth?

Jephthah's Daughter

TAPUAH
Sahalil's lips now have spoken what her eyes told –
She loves me, Amira! My lady fair loves me!
And would this instant – this very now, Amira! –
Take my hand in marriage were I free!
Set me free, Amira – forgo all claims!
[*Gesturing at her abdomen*] I know that thing
Wasn't spawned of my loins, but we could adopt it,
Sahalil and I, if you insist –
But set me free, girl! Set me free!

AMIRA
Some thoughts lately have enraptured my mind…

TAPUAH
Thoughts?

AMIRA
You read me wrong always, Tapuah.
To you I'm the devil's very spawn.
But it is not so. Not so at all.
Envy? Have I envied Sahalil? Who wouldn't!
She has everything – beauty, wealth, grace!
But what churned up envy, turned up love;
I love her, Tapuah, and can't see her miserable.
But I love you too. It won't be easy –
The smile I shall have to give when you wed.

TAPUAH
What? You will free me of your claims?

AMIRA
But I shouldn't be left empty-handed.
Money cannot balm the hurt of losing you,
For I truly love you, Tapuah, but… well –
Underneath the glitz and gold awning
Of friendship with Sahalil, what am I?
What am I but a poor servant girl?
I can't stay forever in Jephthah's house,
And if I leave, what dearest, would I have?

TAPUAH
Amira, I'll give anything you want!
But speak – what I have is yours!
[*Pause.*]

AMIRA
Tapuah?

TAPUAH
[*eagerly*] Yes, Amira?

AMIRA
In your room is a little something
That makes my heart glad to be born.

TAPUAH
What?

AMIRA
A little jade box and its spilling.

TAPUAH
Ah no, Amira! No!
It came from my mother's death-bed!
A family heirloom; jewelery from generations afar!

AMIRA
I see… [*Pause.*] Tapuah…?

TAPUAH
Yes?

AMIRA
Jephthah's East River vineyard
Is hardly matched in all the land.
In beauty and teeming yield,
Not even Abda's grand estates come near.
Hardly, I said, for there is one fair surpassing:
The vineyard called Purple Waters.

TAPUAH
Amira – Purple Waters is a father's gift!
A legacy from my father's father!
Why do you ask the impossible?

AMIRA
[*turning to go*]
You desire the impossible – in marriage.

TAPUAH
Half the vineyard and no more.

AMIRA
All the vineyard,
And need I say all – sweetly all – the jade box?

TAPUAH
Sweet heavens!
She would thrust me into marriage ruined!

AMIRA
Marriage, or the thought of it,
When we aspire askew, is ever ruinous.

TAPUAH
[*turning to back her*] No!

AMIRA
As the failed suitor pleases.
[*She opens the door and slams it without going out, then quickly sneaks behind a nearby curtain.* TAPUAH *turns and hastens to the door.*]

TAPUAH
[*desperately*]
But come, Amira! Come! Have it your way!
[*The door begins to open, and* TAPUAH, *thinking it is* AMIRA *returning, stops and turns away.* SAHALIL *enters.*]
You win! Who makes the rules, wins the game –
It has always been so!
[SAHALIL *coughs and* TAPUAH *turns.*]

Jephthah's Daughter

TAPUAH
Sahalil!

SAHALIL
Does your game
Have room for another? Where is father?

TAPUAH
[*going to door*]
Sahalil, I must fetch Amira!
She shall speak herself to tell and say!
[AMIRA *leaps out of hiding.*]

AMIRA
Yes!

TAPUAH
Amira!

AMIRA
Amira herself says it – It's over!

SAHALIL
Amira, what is this?

AMIRA
A little game, dear, but it's over now.
[*She laughs wildly and pummels her belly.*]

SAHALIL
Stop! Stop! The baby – Amira! Stop! The baby!
[TAPUAH *looks on stupefied.*]

AMIRA
[*stopping*] Where is the baby?

SAHALIL
[*gesturing at* AMIRA's *abdomen*] Amira…

AMIRA
[*twirling round happily*]
Do pregnant maids twirl so prettily?

TAPUAH
You lied? Amira – you lied?

AMIRA
It was just a little game.

SAHALIL
How could you?

AMIRA
I'm not the angel you think me, Sahalil;
Envy stopped by and Jealousy joined her.
But the playing is done and Tapuah yours.

SAHALIL
[*incredulous*] You have loosed him?

AMIRA
Who wants a man
That has no eyes for her? I'd sooner turn my eyes
To little sparkling fires and princely purple glories.

SAHALIL
Such excellency cannot be true! Amira...?

AMIRA
Who liked him anyway? He snores
And needs to scrub underarm a little more.

SAHALIL
[*laughing*]
Oh Amira, you're so terribly silly –
And Sahalil is so terribly happy!
So, so happy! Oh, so happy!
But it can't be true; it can't be!
Oh Tapuah, let's go tell father! Come!
This happening cannot be real...
[The two are close to (R) when JEPHTHAH *enters (L).]*

AMIRA
[*seeing* JEPHTHAH]
But stop! Here is your father!
[SAHALIL *and* TAPUAH *turn.*]

SAHALIL
[*rushing to* JEPHTHAH]
Father – see!
See what has happened, father! See!

JEPHTHAH
What is it, my precious?

SAHALIL
Tapuah and I –
Tapuah and I are getting married!

JEPHTHAH
What!

SAHALIL
[*throwing her arms round his neck*]
Oh father, can such joy be found to live?
I'm going to marry this man!

JEPHTHAH
[*disentangling her arms*] What did you say?

SAHALIL
I have said yes to Tapuah;
The nuptial rose-garland is ours! Oh, father!

JEPHTHAH
[*shaking his head*] My child…

SAHALIL
Father…?

JEPHTHAH
Abda – I have given him consent.

SAHALIL
W-what?

TAPUAH
Sir…!

JEPHTHAH
I asked and you spoke, Sahalil – you spoke!
You said Tapuah's suit was dead. Dead! –
And you would not vary my favor.

SAHALIL
[*stepping back in shock*] B-but… But…
[*Stepping up to* JEPHTHAH]
But I changed my mind, father!
I changed my mind! Father – I changed my mind!

JEPHTHAH
Child, I'm sorry… So sorry… But it's too late.

ABDA
It cannot be too late, sir!

JEPHTHAH
[*threateningly*] Did you say something?

TAPUAH
Sir…
[*He turns away.*]

AMIRA
Surely, Jephthah – you are mistaken?

JEPHTHAH
Am I?

AMIRA
But you said nothing! I saw you –
After you had spoken with Abda, I saw you,
And you said nothing!

JEPHTHAH
You didn't ask.

AMIRA
My lord, you can't do this!

JEPHTHAH
I already have.
Nor may any accuse me of rashness;
For did I not ask Sahalil her choice?
Did I not ask her again and again?

AMIRA
No!

JEPHTHAH
Yes! [*Pause.*] And you, like her,
Blow north and south in one wind.
You favored Abda and now it is Tapuah.
What accounts for this wind?

SAHALIL
Father, you have killed me.
[*Stretching out her hand to* TAPUAH]
Hold my hand, my love – and take me away.
[*As* TAPUAH *stumbles towards her, she breaks into tears and rushes out (R).*]

Jephthah's Daughter

TAPUAH
Sahalil!
[*He rushes out after her.*]

JEPHTHAH
Who can understand the tender gender?
Whose lamp can light the dark of woman?
[*He strides out after them, and* AMIRA *is left alone.*]
[*Long pause.*]

AMIRA
You thought to thwart me – you conspiring air!
And would have! But I am Amira –
Afroth and fertile with asps black and horrid,
Whose grave mistress now mind-ward coils!
Sahalil must burn! *Burn!* And to burn
Must stay all-wombed in Jephthah's household –
Nor marrying Abda, nor marrying Tapuah! –
Nor marrying aught but death in Jephthah's burning!

End of Act1

ACT 2

JEPHTHAH's *house. Lounging chamber as before.*

SAHALIL *is trying some jewelery brought in by* ABDA, *who lounges nearby.*

SAHALIL
So rare, Abda! Rare and lovely!

ABDA
[*moving closer to her*]
How so well it becomes you.

SAHALIL
But from what place of wonder did it come?

ABDA
[*chuckles*]
And now to fetch the dates;
How I forgot them I would never know!
[*Begins to go off.*]

SAHALIL
Ah, but you left them to tease me, you did!
To make me wait when you knew I couldn't wait!

ABDA
And these are special –
Dates spiced, honey from Nectar Valley!

SAHALIL
Oooh! But I can't wait, Abda!

ABDA
[*almost out*]
Won't be a tap and a beat gone.

SAHALIL
[*stopping him*] Abda!

ABDA
My dear?

SAHALIL
[*moving to him*]
The trip to Tyre – when do we set out?

ABDA
I'm calling it off for now.

SAHALIL
[*shocked*]
Calling it off?

ABDA
The ship leaves in three days – not enough time.

SAHALIL
But if you paid the dowry now?

ABDA
Now?

SAHALIL
Today, Abda!

ABDA
The jeweled feast Jephthah demands – it needs time.

SAHALIL
Who needs a jeweled feast, or any feast at all!
Let's catch the ship, Abda; let's spread sail and go!

ABDA
[*hesitantly*]
It's Tapuah, isn't it? You need to be away?
[SAHALIL *turns away silently.*]
When for three days you turned away from me…

SAHALIL
I needed time.

ABDA
To gain strength…

Jephthah's Daughter

SAHALIL
Yes.

ABDA
I knew –
Knew that though your heart was breaking,
Was in shards for Tapuah, the one you love –
Your closeting was not born of rebellion
But was a searching for strength to obey;
To do as you have ever done – obey,
Obey as always your father Jephthah;
And then, Sahalil, I gasped and loved you more.
You see, my dear, though your virtues teem –
Your virtues of grace, beauty, gentleness,
Kindness, innocence – myriad they are!
Yet not these, my dear – not these at all,
From Sahalil's tender years seized my gaze,
But that which to none but a father is virtue:
A deathless obedience, nearing martyrdom,
To who sired you. And when I sat for years
Marveling father-like at such holding devotion,
I rose knowing that you only, Sahalil,
You only, my precious, could be Abda's bride.

SAHALIL
And so I will; but we must brook no delay –
Tyre will have us now. Now, Abda!

ABDA
To you, Sahalil,
I shall be such a husband, I promise,
As would make Tapuah's memory glad to die.

SAHALIL
Yes! But we must be gone to Tyre – a world away…

ABDA
And should Jephthah howl for his jeweled feast –
[SAHALIL *turns awkwardly away.*]
Would you, my dear, in this one thing,
In this one little thing, disobey your father?
[SAHALIL *shifts away, not answering.*]
No, you would not. It is as I feared –
And as I love. Your obedience is to death.
Yet have no fear, Sahalil, my darling;
Jephthah will let us wed, feast or no. He must!
I will go to him, raid him with salted lips!
Besieged by a tongue desperate and apt,
There lives not the man that may not be moved
To a place aslant from his first motion.
[*Begins to go.*]

SAHALIL
Abda…

ABDA
My love…

SAHALIL
Will you forgive me?

ABDA
Forgive you? Forgive you what?

Jephthah's Daughter

SAHALIL
That my heart aches still for Tapuah.

ABDA
My precious…
Let your fears fly in fright and leave you free;
My love for you, like oil from a fallen jar
With no strength to hold back its oiling,
Shall be all the salve your aching heart needs,
Should its pain be thirsty as the sea.

SAHALIL
Forgive me…

ABDA
Man's invention has not uncovered yet
The deed or thought that love may not forgive;
And not as fists clenched, grudging the prizing,
But as feet splayed, happy to dance and leap
To show how deep, how very deep, the love!

SAHALIL
Kind Abda – I'll make you a fine wife yet!
When romantic love plays the truant,
That other love, duty-spawned, duty-bred,
Like a faithful warden, keeps a stern post,
Giving tongue, though starched, though leaden,
To make us do what we must do.

ABDA
Dutiful love, in the wake of happy days,
Oftentimes would shed her warden's starched livery

To don the silk robe of ready love.
And now for the dates, really…
[*Exit.*]

SAHALIL
[*walking back from (R)*]
Ah yes, our dates. I love them…
Or do I not? They were Tapuah's, Tapuah's fancy –
And became mine because they were his.
Tapuah! Oh Tapuah…!
[*Enter* AMIRA.]

AMIRA
What did you say to drive off your betrothed?

SAHALIL
[*abstracted*] What?

AMIRA
But something walks askew here; Abda just fled –
Fled like a bat from a bee's stinging coven!

SAHALIL
Dates.

AMIRA
Dates?

SAHALIL
He's gone to fetch me dates.

AMIRA
[*chuckling*]
Our world crashes about our ears
And all we can find to do is suck dates.

SAHALIL
He said they were special.

AMIRA
Your mind is slewing to a curve, Sahalil.

SAHALIL
You can have them if you want; all of them.

AMIRA
[*shaking her head*]
It is as they say:
Dementia faithfully dogs the heels of heartbreak.
But shake yourself out of this, Sahalil!
Come on! Things will yet turn around; trust me!
[*Enter* JEPHTHAH.]

JEPHTHAH
Where is Abda? I thought he was with you.

SAHALIL
I'm not with him, father.

AMIRA
But of course, my dear. You're with Tapuah.

JEPHTHAH
Amira!
[*He eyes her sullenly.*]

SAHALIL
[*beginning to go off*]
If you want, I'll go fetch him, father.

JEPHTHAH
Why take the trouble? Send someone.

SAHALIL
Trouble? You forget he but lives next door.
[*Exit.*]

AMIRA:
She needn't have gone, but needs the walk;
Abda will be back any moment.
He went to fetch her dates.

JEPHTHAH
Dates!
[*Chuckles*]
I told you it would do the trick –
Tapuah's ban from the house and liaisons;
Now she and the old fellow have fallen
To sucking dates together. Splendid!

AMIRA
She's heartbroken.

Jephthah's Daughter

JEPHTHAH
What nonsense!
She was never in love with Tapuah;
Never had one suitor in mind.

AMIRA
If only you knew…

JEPHTHAH
All I care to know is, what do women want?
When I held myself and gave her the choice,
She refused Tapuah and endorsed Abda.
Then when, acting upon her wishes,
I endorsed Abda and gave him consent,
She said no sire, it is but Tapuah I want.
Is this conduct showing one suitor in mind?

AMIRA
Jephthah, believe me, there is much more to it
Than flashes a straight way eye-ward; much more!

JEPHTHAH
Then say – what color, what form bears much more?
Ceaselessly for three days have you pressed me;
I am sore weary! Sahalil shall marry Abda –
And that's that! Speak no more of it!

AMIRA
And thus – in that very way –
Is your daughter undone and slain!

JEPHTHAH
Enough!

AMIRA
You cannot love her…

JEPHTHAH
Enough, I say! Enough!
[*Walks menacingly to her.*]
I warned you, but would you take heed?
[*Slight pause.*]
As I forbade Tapuah to step foot here,
So now I forbid you from mention ever of him.
Violate this – breach it at peril of your life!

AMIRA
You ban me?

JEPHTHAH
[*most menacingly*]
You doubt me?
[AMIRA *turns away, fearful and silent.*]
Women! Ever seeking to make maids of men!
They would take away our iron
And put in its place brittle sand,
A maggot's spine, the backbone of a worm!
Should Jephthah now eat back his word?
[*Long pause.*]
And yet when you choose, Amira,
Your mind heaves with manly muscle
And wreathes your brow with flowered genius.

Jephthah's Daughter

AMIRA
You will need more than two-faced flattery
To win your way back into Amira's good graces.

JEPHTHAH
But I do not flatter; for is it not true
That in times past when in my troubled breast
Stratagems jostled shark-toothed for dominance,
You ever steered and prodded me right
With insight dazzling enough to shock the fox
And stun the crafty hooded serpent?

AMIRA
For counsel to feed and please your cunning ends,
You would have Amira speak; but to ends
Tethered to plain and simple truth, I am banned.

JEPHTHAH
Leave forbidden territories well alone,
And tell me, Amira, should I or should I not
Bring this certain matter to Abda's disclosure?
It seemed to me right, thinking he was here,
To tell him; but now, not seeing him,
I question the wisdom of being that open.

AMIRA
Tell Abda what?

JEPHTHAH
The feast I would have him give Sahalil
Is naught but a dodge and stratagem of war.
[*Pause.*]

It is simple, really: noise is sounded abroad
Of the grand and jeweled feast impending
To mark the wedding of Jephthah's daughter.
Men of eminence and status in Gilead
And regions round about prepare for the day.
No one – and no one – thinks of war before.
Ammon's sons celebrate their golden chance,
Thinking to alight on the feast day
And strike when Gilead is full of wine and slack.
But Jephthah does not wait. Like a gale,
Like the eagle's swoop, taloned with sudden death,
Jephthah strikes days before – and Ammon expires!

AMIRA
This counsel was given to you by God.

JEPHTHAH
You like it?

AMIRA
God heard your vow,
And gives you now the hammer of destruction.

JEPHTHAH
The wedding feast of Jephthah's daughter…
The grand and jeweled feast…

AMIRA
What stature it now assumes!
Who would think a marriage feast
To grow greater than the wedding it marks?

Jephthah's Daughter

JEPHTHAH
And now that my thoughts are safely ripe,
Should I tell Abda or should I not?
The man has had reasons aplenty
To shun the hop and bustle of a grand feast,
Thinking my stand an offering of vanity.

AMIRA
But give him the reasons you have kissed me with,
And he shall rejoice to have the feast.

JEPHTHAH
Ah, but he shall not have it!

AMIRA
He shall not have it? Now Jephthah,
You take the motion of the culprit worm,
Approbating and reprobating in one swing
And leaving my thoughts miserably boneless.

JEPHTHAH
No – no boneless speech this, Amira,
But the coil of a double ploy,
A fake coin face-up and face-down!
In but the span of three days,
Jephthah shall at night fall upon Ammon,
Sahalil being out of harm's way, well-ensconced
In a ship bound for Tyre, secretly done,
Having been joined to Abda without a feast.

AMIRA
Mmm…

A grand and jeweled feast without a feast –
A dodge wrapped in Cunning's own scarf!
What serpentine coils full-worthy of Amira
Your mind burps, disgorging, Jephthah!

JEPHTHAH
Truly worthy of you?

AMIRA
It is gold, much fine gold…

JEPHTHAH
I'm glad you like it.

AMIRA
I see possibilities …

JEPHTHAH
Teeming and true.

AMIRA
It answers everything.

JEPHTHAH
It answers all, my dear – all!

AMIRA
Yes… Yes… Yes…
[*Enter* ABDA *with a bag of dates.*]

JEPHTHAH
Abda! But hear this, my friend –

Jephthah's Daughter

AMIRA
[*cutting in hastily*] No, Jephthah – no!

JEPHTHAH
B-but you said –

AMIRA
You asked me my thinking; will you not have it?

JEPHTHAH
You said it was gold, much fine gold;
I thought we were done and ready to sell.

AMIRA
A little buffing here and there
Would do our gold no harm, I'm sure.
[*Coaxing* ABDA *out*]
Forgive our too-early display;
A spot of dust on our precious ware
Begs the hand a little buffing.
But stay close, if you will; we'll be selling soon.
[*Exit* ABDA.]

JEPHTHAH
I thought you thought it perfect.

AMIRA
Quite.

JEPHTHAH
Should Abda then not know?

AMIRA
Why should he? To hail and applaud your genius?
True genius prefers to tread the humble path,
Disdaining the allure of self-built monuments.
Besides, no secret is secret once told.

JEPHTHAH
Abda? You think Abda will kite the plan abroad?

AMIRA
What do you know of Abda?

JEPHTHAH
Abda? My trusted friend of years?

AMIRA
Trusted friend, who hides a mother's harlotry
From him who must know, who shares the stain.
[*Pause.*]
Who knows what else hides behind his piety.
Is it not enough he is entrusted
With the hand for life of Jephthah's daughter?
Should Gilead's life, the safety of countless,
Now to Abda be bundled and sold?
Or what is more than life to Jephthah –
Jephthah's heart-leap and ambition?

JEPHTHAH
Hmm.
[*Pause.*]
But the plan –
Without Abda's motion the plan is crippled.

AMIRA
So he would have to know.

JEPHTHAH
Yes.

AMIRA
Eventually – not now. Let's with patience wait
For the ripening of the fruit called Eventually.

JEPHTHAH
Today is all the time we can give Eventually,
If they must be done tomorrow
And journey forth for Tyre's ship.

AMIRA
A day is long enough
When secrets must be told but not too-soon told.

JEPHTHAH
All of today then.

AMIRA
Meanwhile, we must noise abroad the approach
Of Jephthah's daughter's jeweled feast.

JEPHTHAH
One thing remains.

AMIRA
What?

JEPHTHAH
Abda waits.
We boasted loud of gold and shining wares,
But stand market-bare with nothing now to sell
But 'Sorry' and skimpy little lies.

AMIRA
[*chuckling*]
Jephthah of the deeps bested by shallow waters!
[*Coaxing him away (L)*] But go…
Go lest your honest and see-through face,
Unready for skimpy little lies,
Should blush at the sight of naked expedience.
Abda's business is with Sahalil only,
And dates and Amira's counterfeit gold.

JEPHTHAH
My ally and so-sweet reliance.
[*Exit.*]

AMIRA
[*alone*] It is not haven enough
To find Sahalil safety in Abda's house,
But she must find the ships and refuge of Tyre;
While Amira, worthless Amira,
Of use only as Jephthah's kitchen whore,
Must with pots and pans nestle till Victory day –
And then be unshelved to keep Jephthah's vow.
[*Pause.*]
[*Enter* ABDA, *still with the dates. He coughs to attract* AMIRA's *attention, but she remains backing him.*]

Jephthah's Daughter

Abda? I was but this moment leaving to find you.

ABDA
I glimpsed Jephthah crossing the balcony.

AMIRA
Yes, he has gone chamber-ward.

ABDA
But he had something to tell me.

AMIRA
[*most gravely*]
It is I who have something to say.
[*She turns to him, her face a mask of put-on distress.*]

ABDA
Amira! Something troubles you gravely…

AMIRA
Gravely.

ABDA
Is it Sahalil? What has happened to her?

AMIRA
Did you not you see her?

ABDA
See her?

AMIRA
She went after you.

ABDA
What? [*turning to go*] I must go search for her –

AMIRA
[*restraining him*]
No! She is fine, I'm sure.
It's you, Abda, that would bear the probing eye.

ABDA
[*turning to her*] Me?

AMIRA
You.

ABDA
Me!

AMIRA
Tapuah was here.

ABDA
Tapuah?

AMIRA
But a short time ago.

ABDA
He was banned!

Jephthah's Daughter

AMIRA
Jephthah thought it had to do with the war.

ABDA
But it had to do with me?

AMIRA
Yes…
[*Slight pause.*]
Or nearer the truth – your mother.

ABDA
My mother?
[*Drops the bag of dates.*]

AMIRA
Your mother, Abda. *Your mother.*

ABDA
B-but…

AMIRA
How did he know?
[ABDA *is silent. Pause.*]
Secrets! *Tch-tch!* Little devils –
Which on the sudden plague us monster-grown!

ABDA
[*sitting down, crushed*]
How could he know!

AMIRA
Easy –
When jealousy finds desperation.

ABDA
I am ruined.

AMIRA
Only if Jephthah is told.

ABDA
Jephthah does not know?

AMIRA
Jephthah shut him up peremptorily,
Finding his talk wasn't of the drums of war.
But he noised it to me as I shooed him out.

ABDA
And you forsook to tell Jephthah?

AMIRA
Why should I?
Jephthah would never give you Sahalil
If he knew the dung that daubed you;
He wouldn't care to have another harlot
Find room in his whore-spawned house.

ABDA
But you would have me marry Sahalil?

AMIRA
Let's draw the lines, Abda. You've never liked me –
A sentiment well and truly returned;
But I'd rather Sahalil took you than Tapuah.

ABDA
Why? Surely you can't...
[*Pause, staring at her*]
You have an eye for Tapuah!
[AMIRA *turns away.*]
But you and Jephthah, I thought –

AMIRA
[*quickly*]
Jephthah will never marry me! And I'm young –
Yearning like the new-born rose for the sun's kiss.
[*Slight pause.*]
Tapuah once ravished me with talks of love...

ABDA
And if Tapuah cannot marry Sahalil
Because she has known Abda's nuptial kiss,
Tapuah might find Amira once again
To fall upon with love and wedlock talk...

AMIRA
So you see...

ABDA
I do; but Jephthah cannot forever be kept
From Tapuah's sordid destroying tale.

AMIRA
It will find him, but find him late; too late –
If you take Sahalil for wife today.

ABDA
Marry Sahalil today? Impossible!

AMIRA
Today she celebrates her birthday.

ABDA
Yes…

AMIRA
And Jephthah has spoken
Of your little feast to surprise her…

ABDA
Women thrill well to the joy of surprises.

AMIRA
What better day
For a wedding than a maiden's birthday?

ABDA
Yes,
But Jephthah's feast –
The grand and jeweled feast…

AMIRA
Jephthah has changed his mind.

Jephthah's Daughter

ABDA
What!

AMIRA
He worries about Tapuah's bristling
At a time when war itself bristles rabid,
And reasons that Sahalil's sudden marriage
Will of a sudden stop all Tapuah's snarls.

ABDA
Can this be true?

AMIRA
All you need do is dance here dowry-laden.

ABDA
It can't be true…

AMIRA
It is the gold we had to sell.

ABDA
Then why did you have me wait;
Why did you not let Jephthah speak?

AMIRA
If Jephthah had spoken of Tapuah's visit
With some half-churned report, your face, Abda,
Would have spilled your deeds before Jephthah,
As it did you before me, in the dock
Of Tapuah's unfinished story.

ABDA
True… true…

AMIRA
Men without guile should not stroll with their wives
Where their mistresses are apt to visit.

ABDA
Even now, should he bring up Tapuah's visit
When with my dowry and joy I dance forth,
I cannot, Amira, trust my face to lie
And hide what my heart so sadly knows.

AMIRA
Give him no chance;
Confuse his thoughts with gifts and fanfare,
And in the hysteria of tambourines,
Who will remember Tapuah's truncated tale?

ABDA
[*with slow, creeping realization*]
The birthday feast…

AMIRA
Will furnish all the tambourines you need.

ABDA
[*chuckling*]
All is ready then… Everything – ready!

AMIRA
So why wait?

Jephthah's Daughter

ABDA
[*beginning to leave*]
Why wait indeed?

AMIRA
But hearken: Does 'Precipitate' mean secret?
Should Tapuah's madness steal Jephthah's honor
And foreclose the joy of public ado?
Therefore, with courier wings and trumpet voice,
Tell all men high and low, near and far,
That Jephthah's daughter, this very day,
Takes to nuptial breast her lucky lord.

ABDA
My duty needs no spur,
But thank you still, Amira.
[*Exit.*]

AMIRA
[*to empty slipstream*]
And thank you too, my pious fool,
For lending me confederacy's swift hand
In this so sweet and crafty caper.
[*Begins to laugh.*]
[*Enter* SAHALIL.]

SAHALIL
Does laughter in this world still live and breed?
[*Stifling her laugh,* AMIRA *acts as though she is sucking a sweet.*]

AMIRA
[*speaking as though there is a sweet in her mouth*]
It's these sweets.

SAHALIL
What sweets?
[AMIRA *picks up the bag of dates and takes it to her.*]

AMIRA
They touch the palate with spicy song –
[*Opens the bag to offer* SAHALIL *some.*]

SAHALIL
[*peering*] Dates.
[*She turns away.*]

AMIRA
And lift the lips to peppered laugh. Go on; try one.
Who laughs in the face of tragedy,
Whips up reversal and fortune-change.
[SAHALIL *dismisses her with a wave and she dumps the bag, laughing.*]

SAHALIL
I saw Abda dash off.

AMIRA
This is Abda's dashing day
He's gone for more dates – maybe.
[*Breaks into fresh laughter.*]

SAHALIL
And I saw him too!

AMIRA
Saw him too?

SAHALIL
Tapuah.

AMIRA
Tapuah?

SAHALIL
It wasn't him really. It was someone else.
But I thought it was him at first…

AMIRA
Did you run to him?

SAHALIL
No. I just stood there…

AMIRA
And?

SAHALIL
And burst into tears!
Then I saw it wasn't him, but the tears –
The tears wouldn't stop, Amira! And after that…

AMIRA
Poor Sahalil!

SAHALIL
And after that all I could see was him.

AMIRA
Poor, poor Sahalil!

SAHALIL
But I'm much better now.

AMIRA
No, you aren't.
You've got to tell Jephthah, Sahalil;
He can't force you to marry Abda!

SAHALIL
He's not forcing me, Amira.
[*Enter* JEPHTHAH *from (L).*]

JEPHTHAH
Who's not forcing who to do what?
[SAHALIL *turns away in tears.*]
Come now, my precious… What's all this about?
[SAHALIL *remains silent, sniffling.* JEPHTHAH *turns to* AMIRA.] Amira?

AMIRA
She thought she saw him.

JEPHTHAH
Who?

AMIRA
I can't say his name. I'm banned.

JEPHTHAH
Tapuah? Tapuah defied the ban?

SAHALIL
[*hastily*] It wasn't him, father.

AMIRA
Only his unblooded twin.
Now Jephthah must ban all look-alikes of the man.

JEPHTHAH
[*wrapping an arm around* SAHALIL *and moving away with her*]
My dear, you know I love you… Hm?
For you, I would take back my word this minute.
But I am Jephthah. A harlot's offspring – yes!
But Jephthah nonetheless – Jephthah still!
[*Pause.*] Abda keeps faith;
How can I, being Jephthah, break mine?

SAHALIL
Should you have desired
To break faith, I, being Jephthah's daughter,
Would rather kiss death than see it.
[*Breaking away and going towards (L)*]
I'm strong now;
Strong enough, father, to do what I must.

AMIRA
Going chamber-ward?
Then it is as well to change for your feast.

SAHALIL
[*stopping*] My feast?
[*The muted sound of trumpets and tambourines and zithers invade.*]

AMIRA
Listen! Tambourines dance among the trumpets –
Heralding the bangled dancing feet of youths!
Jephthah, can you not hear them?

JEPHTHAH
[*listening*] Yes… Yes…

SAHALIL
I hear them too. What do they portend?

AMIRA
Your feast.

SAHALIL
What feast?

AMIRA
A surprise birthday feast
From the holds and store-rooms of loving Abda.

SAHALIL
Impossible! I'll have no feast, see no one!

Jephthah's Daughter

JEPHTHAH
But you must!

AMIRA
[*leaving*]
I should see how it's all coming, shouldn't I?
[*Exit.*]

SAHALIL
Father, I can't bear a feast; I feel so miserable!

JEPHTHAH
So you need a lift.

SAHALIL
Father, I shall not be there!

JEPHTHAH
You will disgrace me, disappoint my guests?

SAHALIL
You were part of it? Father!

JEPHTHAH
[*chuckling*] Did ever a doting father
Forget his beloved daughter's day?

SAHALIL
Would you believe, father, that I forgot?
Forgot my own birthday, father?
[*Striking her breast*]
Oh father, what turmoil lives here!

JEPHTHAH
Turmoil keeps not house where merriment lives.
But go, my precious, and wash away those tears.

SAHALIL
Father…

JEPHTHAH
But go …
And soon return to give merriment back her house.
[SAHALIL *leaves.*]
[*Singing voices adorn the rising music and*
JEPHTHAH *cocks an ear.*]
But what is this I hear? No music this
For birthdays and common merriment,
But the canticles of nuptial joy!
Wedding feast music! What is this?
[*Enter* AMIRA, *breathless.*]

AMIRA
You won't believe this, Jephthah!

JEPHTHAH
I hear the heralds of marriage…

AMIRA
Abda has gone mad!

JEPHTHAH
The notes of a wedding impending…

Jephthah's Daughter

AMIRA
He comes with his dowry, camel loads of dowry!

JEPHTHAH
The trumpets and cymbals of marriage imminent…

AMIRA
He has set the earth a-merry; all the world claps
That today Abda marries Jephthah's daughter!

JEPHTHAH
My plan… my war plan…

AMIRA
Destroyed!

JEPHTHAH
My golden stratagem…

AMIRA
Yes, I called it gold, for gold it was;
I called it genius, and it was the acme,
The chief and prince of genius!

JEPHTHAH
My inimitable strategy of war;
My grand feast, the jeweled feast
Of Jephthah's precious daughter –

AMIRA
Destroyed and trampled underfoot!

JEPHTHAH
Abda? My friend, Abda?

AMIRA
He took your friendship for granted.

JEPHTHAH
And by that deed joined himself with Ammon.

AMIRA
Yes, indeed.
[*Enter* ABDA, *resplendent in wedding garment.*]

JEPHTHAH
My friend, Abda! My friend!

ABDA
No tongue can spell the joy
That garlands this day's golden brow!

JEPHTHAH
You have brought your dowry, I hear.

ABDA
Yes, my brother, and for once the camels sing,
Happy for their burden, though their backs break.

JEPHTHAH
And the people – they break their throats in song?

ABDA
In all the land and a good measure beyond!

For the couriers of Tob on swiftest saddles
Now ride the wings of my happy command,
Drilling the ear of every nation round about,
With news that Jephthah's daughter this day weds!
O happy me! Happy, happy me!

JEPHTHAH
Woe to me! Wondrous, wondrous woe!
But to Abda more, though he knows it not!

ABDA
Woe? But you brood – You but brood, Jephthah…

JEPHTHAH
You have broken the pact, Abda.

ABDA
Broken the pact? But no…

JEPHTHAH
But yes! Seal my consent with your dowry, said I –
On the day of the feast, the grand and jeweled feast!

ABDA
But Jephthah…

JEPHTHAH
But Abda!
[*He turns in controlled anger and backs* ABDA.
AMIRA, *unseen by the two, then ducks behind a curtain.* ABDA *stands staring stupefied at* JEPHTHAH's *back.*]

ABDA
Jephthah, I can explain…
[*Turning to ask help from* AMIRA] Amira…
[*He gestures in surprise that* AMIRA *is nowhere in sight and turns back to* JEPHTHAH.] Jephthah…

JEPHTHAH
I withdraw my consent.

ABDA
Withdraw your consent?
[*He races to (R).*] Amira! Amira!
[*Racing back to* JEPHTHAH]
No, Jephthah; no, no…

JEPHTHAH
[*rebuffing him*] Yes!

ABDA
Sahalil… but Sahalil is mine…

JEPHTHAH
No more.

ABDA
It cannot be…

JEPHTHAH
I have spoken.

ABDA
[*looking helplessly about*] Amira …

Where is Amira?

JEPHTHAH
Sahalil is free now to entertain other suits!

ABDA
No!

JEPHTHAH
Go!
[*Long silence as* ABDA *gapes at* JEPHTHAH *in disbelief.*]

ABDA
You cannot mean this…

JEPHTHAH
Cannot I? As God lives, the God I serve,
And the God you serve, as He lives, I swear –
I would rather have Sahalil dead
Than married to Abda! Yes, let Sahalil die!
[*He falls to his knees and strikes the floor with his forehead to seal his vow, then rises to his feet.*]
My oath – sealed and done!

ABDA
[*shaking his head*]
Oh this rashness, this rashness…

JEPHTHAH
[*menacingly*]
What says Abda?

ABDA
This rashness – it is madness! Death!

JEPHTHAH
[*approaching* ABDA *with rage*]
You slew my strategy, my golden scheme!
You joined with Ammon to battle Gilead! –
And I refrain from slaying you,
And you call me rash?

ABDA
Slew your strategy? Joined with Ammon?

JEPHTHAH
[*storming at him*]
Go, lest I fall upon you now! Go! Go!
[ABDA *stumbles out.*]
[JEPHTHAH, *facing the audience, tries to gather himself.* AMIRA *emerges from concealment and approaches* JEPHTHAH *with a sly grin on her face.*]

AMIRA
O my one true love…

JEPHTHAH
Amira, why have you delayed
To fetch me my precious daughter Sahalil?

AMIRA
Should I have fetched her?

Jephthah's Daughter

JEPHTHAH
You plague me with foolishness – fetch her!
[AMIRA *begins to go towards (L).*]
Why have I not seen my good man Tapuah?
Where is Tapuah? Fetch me Tapuah!
[AMIRA *changes direction and heads for (R).*]
Where heads Amira? Fetch me Sahalil!
[AMIRA *retraces her steps towards (L).*]
Tapuah! Let him come quick! Fetch him! Fetch him!
[AMIRA *halts, then exaggerates the confusion of commands by comically starting off right then left in quick succession.* JEPHTHAH *turns and sees this, and gawks, thunderstruck. Then* AMIRA *sits down on the floor and begins to suck her thumb, and twine the fingers of her other hand on the edge of her garment, all the while staring innocently at* JEPHTHAH. ABDA *re-enters (R) unnoticed and stays by the door.*]
Amira! What madness enfolds you?

ABDA
It is madness indeed, firstborn and full-tribe –
[JEPHTHAH *and* AMIRA *swivel eyes to him.*]
When men disdain to govern temper or loins!
You cannot deny, friend; no, you cannot,
That I warned and warned, as through the years
Our friendship firmed and grew – I warned and said:
Hot blood, flying, wings not alone
But calls aloft a screech of hot vows,
Which, airborne, spray the earth with blood! –
It is life, innocent life, this thing takes!
Call back your vow, Jephthah! Call back the son

Of foolishness before it takes! Call it back!

JEPHTHAH
You dare?
[*He storms to a sword hanging from a wall and unsheathes it. But when he turns he finds that* ABDA *is gone. He trembles with rage.* AMIRA *rises, at once apprehensive and amused. He considers going for her. She flees. He rages and hurls the sword to the floor in frustration, as lights slowly die.*]

End of Act 2

ACT 3

A lush and tranquil vale, as in Prologue.

Curtains draw open to a dark stage. Nothing is seen.

SAHALIL'S VOICE
Amira! No! No-o-o!
[*A long drawn-out scream. Silence. Then* AMIRA's *voice in gay laughter. Soon joined by* SAHALIL's *voice in gay laughter too. Coming from wings (R) as from some distance away, are the laughing voices of* MAIDS. *Lights grow to daytime brightness.* SAHALIL *and* AMIRA *are now seen laughing in the vale, with the evidence of their picnic lying about. The laughter of the maids begins to die.*]

SAHALIL
I know it's you, but scared stiff I remain.

AMIRA
Is it really me?

SAHALIL
Isn't it?

AMIRA
Is it?

SAHALIL
Of course it is!

AMIRA
Am I really like that? Let's try it again.

SAHALIL
No, Amira, I've had enough.
[AMIRA, *heedless, turns to the audience and is silent and still for a moment, then takes to her face a red mask she had been holding behind her back. It is devilish and terrifying. She turns to* SAHALIL, *who recoils in terror.*]
No, Amira! No!
[AMIRA *removes the mask and begins to laugh.* SAHALIL, *relieved, joins her. Then* AMIRA *whips it back on and turns to wings (R).*]

AMIRA
[*shouting and pointing to her masked face*]
Girls! Who is this? Who?

MAIDS
[*off*] Amira!

AMIRA
[*to* SAHALIL, *removing mask*]
They all think it's me. Maybe it's me.

SAHALIL
[*laughing*] You're silly, Amira; really you are!
[*Stretching happily*]
What a day! What a picnic! And all because of you!
You are a delight, Amira! Such fun!
[*Lights begin to fade to dusk.*]

AMIRA
It's nice to see you happy, Sahalil –
But all because of me? No, Sahalil,
Not me; not me at all, but Tapuah.

SAHALIL
[*throwing her arms in the air*]
O Tapuah! Tapuah! Tapuah!

AMIRA
[*looking about*]
Dusk has stolen quietly on us;
We should leave now, shouldn't we?

SAHALIL
Yes, but what sweet repose my soul finds here;
Would I could lie here forever!

AMIRA
Ever and evermore it will be.

SAHALIL
Oh, to think
Tapuah and Jephthah come tomorrow! –
At dawn, did you say, Amira?

AMIRA
From campaigns east they tent here,
And so will be here when, to hail our heroes,
We show face at the crack of dawn.

SAHALIL
Heroes true!
Oh Amira, how sweet and happy is life!
[AMIRA *suddenly gasps and, tense like a spring, points at a clump of bushes.*]

AMIRA
[*strangled whisper*] See…

SAHALIL
[*terrified*] W-what?

AMIRA
There…

SAHALIL
Where…

AMIRA
[*pointing*] There…

SAHALIL
What?

AMIRA
Ammonites…

Jephthah's Daughter

SAHALIL
Ammonites?

AMIRA
They peep and stare and glower…

SAHALIL
Oh! Flee!

AMIRA
Flee? No! But do as Jephthah and Tapuah did!

SAHALIL
[*desperate, at wings (R)*]
Flee! Flee! Girls! Ammonites! Flee!
[*Amid screams from* MAIDS *off,* AMIRA *leaps at the bushes with war cries and begins to swipe at the empty air.* SAHALIL, *realizing it's a joke, bursts into laughter and is joined by the girls off. She skips to* AMIRA.]
I quite wondered: if Jephthah and Tapuah
Had slain all Ammon, did they then resurrect
To peep and stare and hog up picnic crumbs?

AMIRA
Amira had to have her share of blood.

SAHALIL
[*playing up and gesturing round her*]
And what a share unforgettable!

AMIRA
[*edging close to* SAHALIL]
Yes, Time's offspring will ever recall – this blood.
[*Kisses her.*]

SAHALIL
That was the kiss of – what, pray?

AMIRA
Preparation. A herald of what is to come.

SAHALIL
And what is to come, pray?
[*Pause.*]

AMIRA
Tapuah's kisses.

SAHALIL
[*coyly*] Oh Amira…

AMIRA
But his won't be cheek-bound, mark you.

SAHALIL
Not tomorrow – he dare not! But he can have this –
[*Stretches out her hand with exaggerated aloofness and lets her fingers hang limply.*]
And I'll say – [S*peaking most superciliously*] –
Well, Tapuah, if you must kiss the bride to be – then [*Comically wriggling her fingers*]… innie, minnie, miny, moe.

Jephthah's Daughter

[*They laugh.*]
Now where must I stand tomorrow?

AMIRA
Oh Sahalil, you've forgotten already!

SAHALIL
No, I haven't.
I stand here, and then I run to father
And loop the laurel around his neck.

AMIRA
You're not supposed to be standing!

SAHALIL
Yes, I am!

AMIRA
No! You're in hiding behind the bushes;
How can you be hiding if you're standing?
You've forgotten already, Sahalil;
You've forgotten! Look, this you must do…
[*She goes behind a clump of bushes and crouches down from view, then leaps up with a joyous cry and runs out.*]
[*Momentarily halting*] The mighty Jephthah!
And Tapuah no less a hero – welcome!
[*She continues a little distance, then makes to throw a laurel around someone's neck.*]
[*Returning to* SAHALIL]
You have it now, my dear?

SAHALIL
Would myself had conceived it;
Brilliance dandles on you clever children, Amira!
And the lodging you found close by – how, Amira?

AMIRA
Anything, when the will is resolute,
Is but nothing at all to execute.

SAHALIL
But tomorrow should the girls cough or laugh
As in my hiding-place I pant and wait?

AMIRA
Rest assured; the stage and all its play,
In that great moment, will be yours and yours alone.
[*Lights darken a shade.*]

SAHALIL
Oh, let tomorrow come! Tomorrow hear me,
And ride the swiftest wings of sudden!

AMIRA
It will come, the thing will come;
And when it comes, sudden will break with wonder.

SAHALIL
Let's go. Tomorrow hastens
Only for those who go quick to bed.
[*Calling to wings*] Girls! Girls! Be up and packing!
[*She is busy packing during the ensuing, while* AMIRA *just dawdles about.*]

Amira, oh! – my breast aches, feeling Abda's pain.

AMIRA
Spare him not a moment's pity.

SAHALIL
Oh Amira – such stony hardness
Hardly becomes dear, sweet Amira!
[*Pause.*] Can it be fair
That some should, like the open sky, be glad,
And some, like the slammed jail door, be sad?

AMIRA
Blame Jephthah for it.

SAHALIL
Can we? Father is a wonderful man.

AMIRA
A wonderfully rash man.
[*Pause.*]

SAHALIL
I do admit father does often tread
The too-hasty length of Street Too-Rigid.

AMIRA
Whose pebbles scream and tell the world
That Jephthah is a mightily rash man!

SAHALIL
But it has given Sahalil Tapuah,

The joy and glory of her heart!

AMIRA
And made Abda a very sad man,
Leaving Sahalil's breast aching as hell.

SAHALIL
[*bearing some picnic things*] Let's go, Amira;
Tomorrow may yet kiss away today's sorrows.
[AMIRA, *carrying nothing, swans after* SAHALIL.]

AMIRA
[*calling to wings*]
Girls! Fetch what's left and be along!

SAHALIL
You could give them a hand, Amira.

AMIRA
What are maids for? Let dogs be dogs
And slaves and knaves keep their name.
[*Exeunt, wings (L).*]
[*Dusk lights fade to dark but not to black. Enter* MAIDS *from (R) of a number as in the prologue, laughing and giggling. In the darkness they appear only a little better than silhouettes. Three or four pick up the picnic things left by* AMIRA, *and they all trail out in the direction of the departed two. The laughter of the girls fade with the failing of the lights to black, and in pitch darkness comes the fading up of other sounds from wings (R): the canter of horses, neighs, snorts and stamping of hooves*

Jephthah's Daughter

intermingled with human voices crying out horsy instructions like "Whoa!", "Easy boy!", "Hold there!", "Easy!"]
[*Enter* JEPHTHAH *from (R).*]

JEPHTHAH
A light! A light! Fetch me a light!
[*Enter* SOLDIER *(R) with a light. Stage brightens a bit.* SOLDIER *stands the light, helps* JEPHTHAH *shed his armor and lays him out a sleeping mat.*]
Let Tapuah come once he attends the men.
[*Enter* TAPUAH *(R) as* SOLDIER *bows and turns to leave.*]
Ah, here is the good man! Are the men settled,
  Tapuah?
[*As* JEPHTHAH *and* TAPUAH *talk,* SOLDIER *sheds* TAPUAH *of his armor and lays out his mat before he then leaves (R).*]

TAPUAH
Settled fine for a good night's sleep, my lord,
To greet the town bright-shining tomorrow.

JEPHTHAH
Men touched by heaven as they are,
Should come forth bright-shining ever.

TAPUAH
What awesome shine this victory had!

JEPHTHAH
To be remembered for all time, Tapuah;

And how valiantly played the men their parts,
None bettering you, right hand of mine and son!

TAPUAH
Thank you, my father. Thank you, indeed!
Thoughts of her, my bride-to-be, were all the stay
To play its part, this arm and ax required;
How my heart aches to see my heart's joy!

JEPHTHAH
No more than mine.
Would we could this instant be in Tob to see her –
And the inimitable Amira too!

TAPUAH
Amira?

JEPHTHAH
I kept our liaisons a secret,
Fearing it would but wound Sahalil.
Now happy marriage imminent
Should lend Sahalil tolerance.
Besides, marriage now to Amira
As I propose, seems not too bad a thing.

TAPUAH
Marry Amira?

JEPHTHAH
So she started off as Sahalil's maid,
But is she less a woman for servitude?
Who having eyes to see will deny

Amira bears plenty a woman's charms?

TAPUAH
[*shaking his head in disbelief*]
Did I hear aslant – marry Amira!

JEPHTHAH
What grips you, man?

TAPUAH
Sire, is it of Amira you speak?

JEPHTHAH
Amira.

TAPUAH
No, not Amira.

JEPHTHAH
Amira!

TAPUAH
Amira – the whore?
[*Pause.*]

JEPHTHAH
Whore?

TAPUAH
Whore, sire! Whore!

JEPHTHAH
Amira?

TAPUAH
Amira!

JEPHTHAH
No.

TAPUAH
Yes! Your men – too many I vouch –
Have had their fill of Amira!

JEPHTHAH
Not Amira!

TAPUAH
Amira, sire. I spied on her
And found it was so, so I stopped.

JEPHTHAH
Stopped?

TAPUAH
Yes; I too had business with her.

JEPHTHAH
You? *You?*

TAPUAH
Until no more than a month ago.

Jephthah's Daughter

JEPHTHAH
No... No... No...

TAPUAH
And, sire,
The bed fancy could not lay her on,
The clinking purse did.

JEPHTHAH
Son, speak but plainly.

TAPUAH
A whore she is and a harlot too!
Her legs part too quickly to fancy,
And as quickly to gold and pleasing gifts!
[JEPHTHAH's *head sags onto his bosom. Long silence. Then he erupts.*]

JEPHTHAH
[*thunderously*]
No! No-o-o-o!
[*Long pause, as JEPHTHAH clutches his head as though to contain its explosion. TAPUAH approaches him, stops and clears his throat to attract his attention. JEPHTHAH is heedless.*]

TAPUAH
[*taking a step forward*]
My lord Jephthah...
[*Long pause.*]
My lord, the night thickens and our mats beckon...
[JEPHTHAH *does not stir.*]

Sire…

JEPHTHAH
[*waving him off*]
Find sleep, Tapuah;
I will yet ponder this failing of the light.
[TAPUAH *waits a while then slouches away to find sleep on his mat. Soon he is snoring in sleep, and* JEPHTHAH *has begun to pace. He stops.*]
Not just a whore, but in the selling end – a harlot…
[*An owl begins to hoot. He resumes his pacing. He stops.*]
Not just… Not… Not… Not just…
[*Shakes his head.*]
I shared my bed, offered my heart…
I, Jephthah, took her – and what was she?
A common harlot! Slime-gob of womanhood,
To be bought and sold and market-haggled!
Has the wide world not space enough
To flee the stain and name of harlot?
[*He resumes his pacing, as the torch wanes and the owl's hooting intensifies. Suddenly a long wail comes from the sleeping* TAPUAH. JEPHTHAH *goes to him and observes him for a while, but there is silence. He turns and begins to move off but is stopped by a loud sobbing sound from* TAPUAH *which causes him to turn again to his sleeping lieutenant.*]
Tapuah! You sob! Tapuah!
[TAPUAH *does not stir, but the sobbing diminishes.*]
[*Turning and going off*] What dream-monsters
The warrior crops from war, even the best of

soldiering men...
[*The torch fails to a little more than a glow, and with the greater darkness comes an intensification of the owl's hooting to almost fever pitch.*]
Silence! Accursed thing! Silence!
Foul bird of death and grief – silence!
[*The owl appears to obey and there is a sudden hush.* JEPHTHAH *goes to his mat and as he prepares to lie down there is a terrifying screech and a flurry of wings about his head.*]
[*Beating off the bird*]
Begone, bird of doom! Begone! Begone!
[*He chases the fleeing bird a pace or two.*]
[*Returning*] This vale was once a place of peace...
[*Another dreadful screech suddenly breaks the silence as another owl attacks* JEPHTHAH.]
[*Beating it off*]: Away! Away!
Find your mate and perish! Away!
[*The bird flees in the direction of the first.*]
This place swarms with birds of death;
When did death flee the fields of war
To haunt this once restful vale?
[*He lowers himself down on his mat and stretches out for the night. There is a hush except for distant, non-threatening hooting of the owls. Soon* JEPHTHAH *begins to snore. Suddenly a heart-rending wail rents the air.* JEPHTHAH *wakes and leaps to his feet. Realizing it is* TAPUAH, *he rushes to him and tries to shake him awake.*]
Awake, man! Awake! Tapuah!
[*Slight pause.*] Tapuah! What sleep is this
That grips you like death's twin?

Tapuah! Awake, man! Awake!
[TAPUAH *stops wailing, wakes, but wakes with sobbing tears. He sits up, trying to stem his sobbing.*]
Tapuah, what is this?
What dream has bested you?
You wail, you cry and will not wake.
What is the matter, man?
[TAPUAH *just sits, staring at him.*]
Tapuah, what visions spawn you terror?
[*Enter* SOLDIER.]
Why? Inhabit deep your bed again, soldier!
Wait! – Say nothing of this – for all is well!
[SOLDIER *bows and leaves.*]
Or do I, Tapuah, lie and speak not well?
[TAPUAH *rises to his feet and paces about. JEPHTHAH stares at him.*]
[*Approaching him*] Tapuah…

TAPUAH
Sire, do not bid me relate the horror,
Lest speaking should flesh and bring it on us!
No, sire, let it die! Let it but die!

JEPHTHAH
Wars birth strange visions.

TAPUAH
Would to heaven this were war's mischief,
Illusory images of war's labors!

Jephthah's Daughter

JEPHTHAH

It is, and nothing to summon worry.
We are God's battle-ax; tears do not become us.
[*Going to his mat*]
Let us to bed and be men; tomorrow comes.
[JEPHTHAH *lies down in repose. After a while*
TAPUAH *goes to his mat.*]

TAPUAH

Yes, let us be men.
[*He lies down for a moment; then sits up shaking his head. Spotlight on his face streaming silently with tears. After a bit the glowing torch fails simultaneously with the spotlight. Pitch darkness. The hooting of owls in the distance. Long pause. The lights grow gently to signify dawn, and to reveal* TAPUAH *still sitting up. He rises to his feet and begins to tidy himself up.* JEPHTHAH *rouses too. Their talking is done as they tidy themselves up.*]

TAPUAH

Good morning to you, my lord.

JEPHTHAH

A fair morning, indeed, after the dreadful night.
I dreamed of horsemen – five! – in a desperate race,
Whose end was no end but its beginning!

TAPUAH

Five horsemen?
You sent five men yesterday on horseback to Tob.

JEPHTHAH
I know, I know.

TAPUAH
Why, sire?

JEPHTHAH
To keep Sahalil and Amira
From meeting me till I deem fit.

TAPUAH
What spurred the confining, sire?

JEPHTHAH
A vow.

TAPUAH
A vow?

JEPHTHAH
The vow I made.

TAPUAH
You vowed not to see them?

JEPHTHAH
I vowed that if I had victory I would give
As burnt offering the first from my house
Who came to me in greeting and welcome.

TAPUAH
No, sire, surely you didn't vow that?

JEPHTHAH
So I did.

TAPUAH
But surely you couldn't have meant it?

JEPHTHAH
I meant it. And still do.

TAPUAH
Sahalil –

JEPHTHAH
Sahalil was to be in Tyre,
A sea and a world away with Abda;
But fret not, the horsemen will serve duty.

TAPUAH
Only if Amira knows not the vow.

JEPHTHAH
Amira?

TAPUAH
Amira is none but Evil's firstborn;
Envy and murderous hatred ride the blood
Her black and hellish heart feeds her mind!
She begs but chance to do Sahalil in!

JEPHTHAH
She was there; Amira heard the vow.

TAPUAH
The dream! No!
[*He dashes away (R).*]
[JEPHTHAH *contemplates for a moment, then strides after him. Enter* SAHALIL *from (L) with two laurels and a horn around her neck.*]

SAHALIL
[*looking around*]
Their mats mark them here;
They are here – but where?
[*She then hears the voices of* JEPHTHAH *and* TAPUAH *offstage as they approach, and ducks behind the bushes as arranged.*]

TAPUAH
[*off, approaching*]
But you should have sent me, sire – not the five;
No errand more deserves my embassy!

JEPHTHAH
[*off, approaching*]
Keep your cool, Tapuah, my boy; easy!
You need a clear head to race well.
[*They enter.*]

TAPUAH
I shall race the wind sorry and breathless!

JEPHTHAH
From the brow of Hassock, go by Guha;
It will save you a long and scraggy ride.

Jephthah's Daughter

TAPUAH
[*shouting towards wings (R)*]
The steed! How long to ready a horse?

JEPHTHAH
But we fret needlessly; Sahalil is safe with the five.
[SAHALIL *springs up from her concealment.*]

SAHALIL
[*with a great smile*]
Not with any five,
But in a father's hands, is Sahalil safe!
[*Leaping out and running to the dumbstruck* JEPHTHAH]
Mighty Jephthah – hero unequaled!
[*Hugging him*] Welcome, my father!
[*Slipping a laurel around his neck*]
Welcome, Prince of Gilead!
[*Going to* TAPUAH *with the second laurel*]
And Tapuah whose exploits fill Tob with song...
[*She wreathes him and glances into his face.*]
Tapuah? What sorrow unmatched mottles your face?
[*Turning and finding* JEPHTHAH *equally grief-stricken*] And you, father...
[*Turning back to* TAPUAH] This is grief unutterable.
[*Turning to* JEPHTHAH] Father...

TAPUAH
[*in a strangled voice*]
Why is Amira not coupled here with you?
[SAHALIL's *distress finds relief and she begins to chuckle.*]

SAHALIL
[*turning to* JEPHTHAH]
Oh Papa, what dark secrets you keep!
But I wasn't cross when it slipped Amira's lips –
Well, not more than from lunch to supper-time.
How can anyone as happy as I
Be cross a full day? A double wedding!
Oh Papa, you and Amira are perfect fit!

TAPUAH
Where is Amira?

SAHALIL
[*glancing from one man to the other*]
But stop! Did you really think I would harm her?
Yes, bothered and confused I was at first –
How one maid can play two fires staggers me –
But I didn't think to rage or scratch her eyes!

TAPUAH
Where is she?
[SAHALIL, *rather miffed at the apparent distrust, takes her horn to her lips and blows. There is an eruption of jubilation from offstage (L). Shouts and laughter and music. A band of women and children, with* MAIDS, *troop in, dancing and singing. Enter* AMIRA *alone, dancing.*]

JEPHTHAH
[*bellows, grief-stricken*] Amira!
[*The merriment stops. Silence.*]
The vow!

Jephthah's Daughter

AMIRA
Vow? What vow?

JEPHTHAH
You let Sahalil come!

AMIRA
What is my lord teeth-gnashing about?

JEPHTHAH
The vow!

AMIRA
But what vow, my lord? What vow?

JEPHTHAH
You heard it! Who greets me first from my house
When I have trampled Ammon and come victorious,
Will strap the altar, a burnt sacrifice!

AMIRA
[*hand flying to her mouth*]
Oh no! No! No!

JEPHTHAH
You let Sahalil come!

AMIRA
My lord, I quite forgot – I but swear it!
Surely, you do not intend it still?

TAPUAH
[*going to her*] It is as well, Amira,
That Jephthah recoiled and took back his word.

AMIRA
[*stepping forward to* JEPHTHAH *in shock*]
What? You took back your word?

JEPHTHAH
So you remembered.
[*Now by* AMIRA, TAPUAH *in one swift motion unsheathes his dagger.*]

TAPUAH
[*stabbing her in the stomach*]
Yes, she did, and so she died;
For devils, however fiendish, must expire and fall!
[*He moves away. Silence as all watch in shock as* AMIRA *staggers about with the dagger in her.*]

SAHALIL
T-Tapuah… you – you stabbed her?

TAPUAH
No more sly or wicked fiend
Did Hell's orifice excrete.
[SAHALIL *leaps to* AMIRA *as she falls face down in death.*]

SAHALIL
Girls, help her! Help her!

TAPUAH
[*leaping forward with drawn sword*]
Back! Back! Everybody, back! Let no one touch her!

SAHALIL
Father, but intervene! Tapuah has gone mad!
[*Enter* ABDA, *unseen by* JEPHTHAH, SAHALIL *or* TAPUAH.]

JEPHTHAH
No, he has not; he has only slain the devil –

SAHALIL
Father!

JEPHTHAH
Who has killed you…

TAPUAH
[*stepping up to* JEPHTHAH]
Surely your word is annulled,
Seeing it is Sahalil?

SAHALIL
Killed me?
[*Bending to* AMIRA]
Amira, sweetest friend, It cannot be as they say?

JEPHTHAH
[*gently pulling* SAHALIL *away*]
Come away, my child,
From she who has taken your life…

TAPUAH
No, Jephthah – no!

ABDA
No, not Amira!
Not she has taken Sahalil's life, but Jephthah!

JEPHTHAH
[*turning and seeing him*] Abda…

ABDA
Amira was evil, and evil must do as evil does,
But only can, when men give her room and board,
Which you did by temper and reckless word.

TAPUAH
But Jephthah cannot keep his vow;
Tell him, Abda! Tell him!

ABDA
Jephthah…
[JEPHTHAH *turns away from them and faces the audience. He stares long and hard. Lights fade to black, leaving only a spotlight on him.*]

JEPHTHAH
I am Jephthah. As I have vowed, so I must do;
I cannot take back my word.
[*He falls to his knees with a great groan, rending his clothes and tearing his hair and wailing.*]
[*A great bellow*] Woe! Woe! Woe is me! O woe!
[*Spotlight fails. Black.*]

Jephthah's Daughter

SAHALIL'S VOICE
As you have vowed, my father, so do to me;
Only give me two months to roam the mountains,
Weeping and bemoaning my virgin death.
[*Lights rise and grow to dim. Only* SAHALIL *and her* MAIDS *are on stage, as in the prologue, with* MAIDS *in a circle covering a supine* SAHALIL *from view. They part and* SAHALIL *is seen.*]

MAIDS
[*in dirge*]
The tongue kills as surely as thrust of blade
Here – O here! – lies one slain by the tongue
Here is she killed by curve of mouth
Here is she slain by careless word
O here – here lies one slain by the tongue!

JEPHTHAH'S VOICE
Give your servant victory and Jephthah vows –
Your servant Jephthah vows, O God of gods –
Grant victory unto me and I shall give
The first, as burnt offering, O God – the first
From my house that comes to me upon my return!
Yes, O God – who comes first from my house
I shall give to you as burnt offering!

MAIDS
[*in dirge*]
The tongue kills as surely as thrust of blade
Here – O here! – lies one slain by the tongue
Here is she killed by curve of mouth
Here is she slain by careless word

O here – here lies one slain by the tongue!

JEPHTHAH'S VOICE
[*off*] My daughter, is it you?

SAHALIL
[*half rising*] What is it, my father?

JEPHTHAH'S VOICE
[*off*] O woe! Woe! Woe is me!
[*Pause.*]
I am Jephthah. As I have vowed, so I must do;
I cannot take back my word.
[SAHALIL *rises.*]

SAHALIL
[*in dirge*]
Do to me, father, as you have vowed
For you are Jephthah
And I'm your daughter
Of the tribe that keep their word
Even to the death
Of the tribe that keep their word
That keep their word
Even to the death
Of the tribe that keep their word
Even to the death
Lo! I shall never know sweet wedlock
Never know the arms of nuptial warmth
But among the lilies
In the high mountain crags
A maid of maids

Jephthah's Daughter

Virgin to the death
I shall roam
For I am of those that keep their word
That keep their word
Even to the death
Those that keep their word
Even to the death
[SAHALIL *lies down again.*]

MAIDS
[*in dirge*]
The tongue kills as surely as thrust of blade
Here – O here! – lies one slain by the tongue
Here is she killed by curve of mouth
Here is she slain by careless word
O here – here lies one slain by the tongue!
[*Repeating the dirge, they troop off the stage,
leaving* SAHALIL *spotlighted as general lights fail.
Then spotlights fail, with dirge still continuing. Then
silence.*]

The End

www.ingramcontent.com/pod-product-compliance
Lightning Source LLC
Chambersburg PA
CBHW031632160426
43196CB00006B/382